W9-ATD-121

131 Creative Strategies for Reaching

Children With
Anger Problems

A practical resource of approaches and activities
for helping chronically angry children (K-8).

By Tom Carr, M.S. L.P.C.

© 2000 by
YouthLight, Inc.
Chapin, SC 29036

Cover Illustration - Walt Lardner
Layout & Design - Melinda Boyle & Melissa White
Layout & Design Supervisor - Elizabeth Madden
Project Editing - Susan Bowman
Project Supervisor - Susan Bowman

ISBN
1-889636-20-7

Library of Congress
99-66151

10 9 8 7 6 5 4 3 2
Printed in the United States of America

Dedication

To Bill McCormick, my principal,
co-worker for nearly 15 years.

Thanks for your constant support & encouragement.

About the Author

Tom Carr lives in Hillsborough, North Carolina with his wife, Carlye. He holds a Master's Degree in Counseling and Guidance from Syracuse University and is a National Board Certified Counselor and a Licensed Professional Counselor. He has been a school counselor for twenty years and presently works for Orange County Schools in North Carolina. He also owns his own private practice, Carr Counseling & Consultation, Inc. and he is an educational consultant for Developmental Resources, Inc. in Chapin, South Carolina. In 1999 Tom created The Strength Coaching Foundation in his community which helps provide financial support for children with special gifts, strengths, and talents. Tom has presented hundreds of workshops across the country for parents, counselors, and teachers. He has written several books including, *Keeping Love Alive in the Family, Monday Morning Messages, A Parents Blueprint,* and *Every Child Has a Gift.*

Table of Contents

Preface i

Section 1: Understanding Anger 1

    What is Anger?...1

    The Effects of Anger 2

    The Causes of Anger 5

    Roadblocks to Anger Management 10

Section 2: The 131 Creative Strategies and Suggestions 15

    Level 1: Mild Anger (Strategies 1-32) 16

    Level 2: More Challenging Anger (Strategies 33-65)...........38

    Level 3: Extreme Anger (Strategies 66-108) 58

    Level 4: When Nothing Else Works (Strategies 109-130) 77

    Tips For Parents Of An Angry Child (Strategy 131) 87

Appendices 95

    Appendix A: Criteria For ADD/HD 95

    Appendix B: Criteria For Conduct Disorder 96

    Appendix C: Criteria For Oppositional Defiant Disorder 98

    Appendix D: Anger Disorders...99

    Appendix E: A Teacher's List of Do's & Don'ts On Medication 101

    Appendix F: Recommended Resources On Anger

                 and Related Topics...103

References 105

Preface

Years ago Charles H. Spurgeon noted, "Anger is temporary insanity." For most people, bouts of anger are temporary. For children, anger is quite common as they learn to deal with life's frustrations. Many children learn how to cope with anger at a young age while others will take several years to finally gain self-control. The children that struggle need to be surrounded by caring and patient adults who are willing to teach anger management skills and who also model positive ways of dealing with anger.

This book will provide counselors, teachers, parents, and other professionals numerous strategies for reaching children with anger problems. Although this book can be useful with children of all ages, I focused on those in grades K-8.

The first section provides the reader with a better understanding of anger: its causes, effects and roadblocks to anger management. Section 2 contains 131 practical strategies and suggestions. Included in this section are 24 skillsheets that can be copied/reproduced to help teachers, parents, and the children. The last strategy is designed especially for parents. It is written in such a way that it can be used as an outline for a five-session parenting workshop.

The last section is the Appendices. It contains criteria for several disorders such as Attention Deficit Disorder, Conduct Disorder, and Oppositional Defiant Disorder. Also included are five other basic anger disorders, a list of Do's and Don'ts concerning medications and a listing of other helpful resources on the topic of anger.

131 Creative Strategies for Reaching Children with Anger Problems

Section 1 – Understanding Anger

What is Anger?

According to Marian Marion (1994), "Anger is an emotion, an effective state or feeling experienced when needs are frustrated or when well-being is threatened. Anger is emotional energy that can motivate a person to attempt to remedy the situation that brought on the anger." (p. 156) In the book, *Mind, Body, Health* (1996), author Brent Hafen takes his definition of anger from expert Carol Tavris who reported, "Anger is an emotion that is temporary and it combines physiological arousal with emotional arousal. It can range in severity all the way from intense rage to cool anger that doesn't really involve arousal at all (and might more accurately be described as an attitude, such as resentment)." (p. 170) Diane Tice (1993) found that anger is the mood most people are worse at controlling. Paul Ekman (1974) listed anger as one of the six basic prototypical human emotions, along with sadness, happiness, fear, surprise, and disgust, that all human's experience regardless of culture.

Anger is a powerful and dangerous emotion. Author and psychotherapist, Bill Borcherdt (1989) noted, "Of all the human emotions, anger has created the most harm and caused the greatest destruction within individuals, couples, families, and between social groups and nations." (p. 53) The famed Duke University researcher Redford Williams authored the book *Anger Kills* (1993). He noted, "Anger

1

kills…we're speaking here not about the anger that drives people to shoot, stab, or, otherwise wreak havoc on their fellow humans. We mean instead the everyday sort of anger, annoyance, and irritation that courses through the minds and bodies of many perfectly normal people." (p. xiii)

Terms that deal with anger are more and more common in the English language. There are numerous anger metaphors used today. Here are a few that I'm sure you've heard before: You make my blood boil, letting off steam, doing a slow burn, getting hot under the collar, simmer down, reached the boiling point, seething with rage, ticked-off, fuming, like a pressure cooker, anger bottled up inside, blew a fuse, blew my stack, breathing fire, burned up, anger welled up inside, bursting with anger, she flipped her lid, he hit the ceiling.

Even in our schools today we are using labels and terms that deal with angry children that were unheard of twenty or thirty years ago. They include defiant, compulsive, inflexible, explosive, problems shifting gears, mean spirited, Attention Deficit/Hyperactivity Disorder, Conduct Disorder, and Oppositional Defiant Disorder. Out in the street you hear people talking about road rage, drive by shootings and Type A personalities. Movies are filled with violence and much of today's music contains offensive and violent lyrics. Unfortunately, anger plays a major role in our society.

The Effects of Anger

Anger affects all facets of society. In this section I will focus on four areas: crime, interpersonal relationships, health issues and how anger hinders the teaching and learning that takes place in our schools today.

1. Crime

Crime affects many people and the most serious crimes are commited by those who can't control their anger. Although murder rates have dropped recently, the United States still has the highest homicide rate of any Western industrialized country. Novello, Shosky, and Froehike (1992) found that homicide is the second leading cause of death among 15 to 24-year-olds. Research by Leonard Eron (1994) documents that by age eight, boys' patterns of aggressive behavior and attitude are already crystalling, so much that without intervention such patterns tend to continue into adulthood. Several years ago Huesmann, Eron, Lefkowitz, and Walder (1984) also noted that aggression present as early as age eight predicts criminal behavior at age 30 (e.g., arrests, convictions, traffic offenses, DWI's, spouse abuse).

2. Inter-Personal Relationships

Anger interferes with positive communication between individuals. Poor communication is the number one cause for divorce in our country. Friends, co-workers, neighbors, family members, and classmates allow anger to hurt relationships.

3. Health Issues

People who fail to control their anger are putting themselves in a dangerous situation. A study by the American Heart Association stated that people who can't keep their tempers under control and who tend to explode in anger during arguments double their risk of heart attack. (Hafen, 1996) Duke University's Redford Williams informs us several times in his book *Anger Kills* that there is strong evidence that hostility alone damages the heart (1993). Many researches agree that the number one cause of death in America – coronary heart disease – is related to anger. Hafen (1996) tells of a study that took place at the University of Michigan conducted by Mara Julius that showed that a person with high blood pressure who suppresses anger, is five times more likely to die than is a high blood pressure victim without suppressed anger. It appears obvious that people of all ages are at risk if they do not learn to manage anger effectively.

There are several physiological responses to anger besides high blood pressure and heart disease. Anger causes increased heart rate, increased general muscle tension, trembling or shaky hands, sweaty or clammy hands, rapid breathing, reddening of the skin or hot sensations, restlessness or agitation, jumpiness or exaggerated startle reactions, feeling hyperaroused, stomach pain or nausea, grinding of teeth, scowling or glaring, goose bumps, chills, shudders, prickly sensations, numbness, choking, twitching, sweating, and headaches. Other common reactions associated with chronic anger include pain in the neck, ringing in the ears, lowered skin temperature, hives, acne, migraine headache, hiccuping, peptic ulcers, chronic indigestion, diarrhea, constipation, intestinal cramping, loss of appetite and frequent colds.

4. Teaching and Learning

Anger interferes with many children's ability to learn. Angry students often keep teachers from teaching. As professionals we need to identify these angry children at an early age. The earlier we get involved, the sooner we can help them. Much research has been completed over the years that helps us to look for signs and cues that tell us which children are headed for trouble in school and in society. Buntaine and Costenbader (1997) report, "The belief that early aggressive behavior places children at-risk for negative outcomes is substantiated by empirical research." (p. 626) Buntaine and Costenbader also note that those children who display extreme levels of aggression at an early age are more likely to require higher levels of mental health intervention, more likely to become juvenile delinquents, have higher rates of school drop out, demonstrate lower levels of academic achievement and be rejected by their peers.

In the book, *Lost Boys*, author James Garbarino (1999) provides us with an example of how early intervention with very young boys can "turn them around." He reports on a study conducted by psychologist Sheppard Kellan at Johns Hopkins University in 1998. The study found that violence prevention programs and effective classroom management techniques in *first* grade can have a dramatic effect on the likelihood than an aggressive six-year-old will become a violent thirteen-year-old. Garbarino writes, "Kellams' group found that highly aggressive six-year-old boys placed within well-managed first grade classrooms run by effective teachers were three times less likely to be highly aggressive by the time they reached eighth grade than similarly aggressive boys who were placed in a chaotic classroom with ineffective teachers." (p. 66)

The Causes of Anger

Anger has many causes. Some causes are easy to identify. For example, eight year-old Marcus knocks over some books and slams the phone down. His father just informed him that he would not be able to attend tonight's youth basketball game. Marcus loudly responds, "That's the third time this week he didn't keep his promise!" Other times finding the cause of a child's anger is almost impossible. Quite often a child really doesn't know why he/she is angry. Have you ever asked a five year-old, "Why are you so angry?" and the child replies, "I don't know."

Ben Franklin said, "Anger is never without a reason, but seldom a good one." There are numerous reasons and causes why children get angry. I like to call these reasons and causes, "Anger Avenues." They are the pathways to anger problems and they can be biological/genetic or environmental.

1. Childhood Stressors

All children encounter "stressors" at home and school. These stressors can lead to temporary or situational anger. In their book, *Childhood Stress (1990)*, authors Susan Jones Sears and Joanne Milburn write, "School aged children are understandably stressed by many of the same things that stress pre-schoolers--divorce of parents, serious illness that requires hospitalization, or witnessing violence. But when school enters the picture, so does a whole new host of stressors. According to researchers, the most common stressors of school-aged children include: anxiety about going to school, bullies, changing schools, conflicts with the teacher, forced competitiveness, difficulty with classmates, failing to make an athletic team, having to give oral reports in front of class, learning disorders, being unable to complete homework assignments, lack of parental interest in achievements, parental pressure to achieve, dealing with the reputation of older siblings (good or bad), worry about taking tests, and even special recognition (for making honor roll, winning a debate). A significant amount of stress stems from peer teasing--about being over weight, being of a different race, wearing glasses, having red hair, wearing dental braces, and so on." (p. 231)

© 2000, YouthLight, Inc.

2. Too Strict or Harsh Parenting

An important finding of a George Washington University study (Hamer, 1998) is that negative parenting has a statistically stronger effect-causing bad behavior than positive parenting causing good behavior. "Occasionally blowing up at a child, or even a well-deserved spanking, is not going to do permanent damage. The danger is slipping into negative habits, into a pattern of negative parenting toward a child, because bad parenting is what has the strongest impact." (p.122) Houston & Vavak (1991) found that students who were most hostile seemed to have had an "oppositional orientation" toward people that developed during childhood. They came from homes where both parents were strict and coercive, used frequent physical punishment or hostile control, and frequently communicated dissatisfaction with the child. Those who scored high on hostility, described parents who were less warm and accepting, less likely to have encouraged independent thinking. Those who were the most hostile, were also those with the lowest self-esteem and the greatest levels of anger.

Hamer (1998) wrote, "Sadly, the parents who have by far the biggest influence on their children are the ones who beat and abuse them. The impact is well documented and undeniable, and always negative. The effects are apparent early on: kindergartners were twice as likely to be aggressive if they were abused at home. And the damage lasts forever. Children who were identified by courts as having been abused or neglected were 42% more likely to be arrested for violence as adults than people who were raised without abuse." (p. 122)

3. Inconsistent Parenting

Parents who consistently change their parenting styles often confuse and anger their children.

4. Poor Role Modeling by Parents

Children often imitate their parents. If they view their parents venting anger inappropriately, they may do the same. Some children have parents who are incarcerated or constantly in trouble with the law. These children will sometimes look to their peers as role models.

5. Parental Expectations too High

Many parents are guilty of setting unfair expectations for their children. When the children realize they can't fulfill their parents' wishes, they give up, rebel, or turn angry. Many children are expected to live out their parent's dreams that they were never able to reach.

6. Troubled Neighborhoods

Children living in "tough" neighborhoods with bullies, gangs, drugs, and crime have to develop a "tough" attitude to survive. Dean Hamer notes, "Of all the things that determine whether people will be violent, aggressive, and antisocial, the most important factor is not the type of brain a person has or whether they were abused as children. What matters most is geography." (p. 123) Hamer was referring to neighborhoods. Judith Harris, in her book, *The Nurture Assumption* (1998) wrote, "You don't have to do anything quite that drastic (move to another country) to have an effect on your child's life. Just by moving to a different neighborhood, just by choosing your child's school, you can change the course of life. It's a little scary, isn't it...on the whole, children learn more in schools that contain a higher proportion of smart kids; on the whole, children are less likely to get into trouble in neighborhoods where delinquency rates are low." (p. 212) British studies have shown that when delinquent London boys move out of the city their delinquency rate declines even if they move with their families. Buntaine & Costenbader (1997) studied children who lived in urban, rural, and suburban areas. Their research centered around expressions of anger. Children in urban areas reported the most problems expressing and dealing with anger. The researchers also reported that location had more effect on children's individual responses to anger than did gender. Analyzed by location, urban children reported significantly higher levels of anger than suburban or rural children. Urban children were less able to discriminate between accidental and intentional acts that provoked anger.

7. Fears/Grief and Loss

Children may have certain fears or anxieties. They have the potential to explode when faced with their fears. Many children also have unresolved grief due to loss. Some children face several losses before they reach the fifth grade. These children may become stuck in the anger stage of grief.

8. Social Skills Deficit

Many children enter school minus important social skills. They don't know how to use good manners, how to be patient, take turns, work in groups, how to properly ask for something, or how to use appropriate voice levels. These children find it difficult to get along with others and tend to get frustrated and angry. Many of these children lack empathy. Their parents may actually encourage aggression. Education expert, James Comer noted (1988), "Expectations at home and school may be radically at odds. For example, in some families a child who does not fight back will be punished. And yet the same behavior will get the child in trouble at school." (p. 5)

9. Non-Verbal Learning Disabilities

Often students with learning disabilities get so frustrated that they explode. Matt tries and tries to complete a long division math problem. He can't get the correct answer and finally loses it. He rips up his worksheet and throws it on the floor. Many LD children use up all their energy "holding it together" at school and then when they get home they "let it out."

10. Difficult Temperaments

Some children have such a personality or temperament that makes them short-fused, more irritable and moody, and easily frustrated. Other children are easy-going, constantly in a good mood, and always willing to please. If you have children of your own you've come to realize that each one has his/her own personality. Are children so different because of parenting or are some children just "born that way?"

Research completed with identical twins separated at birth by Thomas Bouchard (1990) found, "One of the most surprising things in our study, which is really quite consistent with a lot of the twin and adoption work, is that almost, as far as we can tell, all personality traits are influenced about 50% by genetic factors and 50% by environmental factors." (p. 634) William Wright in his book, *Born That Way* (1998) wrote, "Genes influence not just physical characteristics such as hair color and susceptibility to cancer but our personalities, temperaments, behavioral patterns, even personal idiosyncrasies, the quirks and foilbles that make each person unique." (p. 5)

In an article that was printed in the December 2, 1986 *New York Times* describing research completed at the University of Minnesota, author Daniel Goleman, who later wrote the book *Emotional Intelligence*, started the newspaper article by saying, "The genetic make up of a child is a stronger influence on personality than child rearing, according to the first study to examine identical twins reared in separate families." He went on to write, "For most of the traits measured, more than half the variability was found to be due to heredity, leaving less than half determined by the influence of parents, home environment, and other experiences in life." (p. 54) Dean Hamer (1998) notes in his book, *Living With Our Genes*, "Another myth about aggression is that angry people are solely the product of a bad childhood or bad neighborhood, or that loving parents can keep any child from growing up violent. These theories are based on a misunderstanding of how the brain works and the nature of human temperament." (p. 91)

We could argue the "nature vs. nurture" theory for hours but, more and more research is finding that a good portion of a child's temperament is inherited. We can't put all the blame on parenting.

11. Sensory Integration Dysfunction

Some children have difficulty integrating various sensory systems such as touch, movement, coordination, body position and awareness. These children may overreact to loud noises, bright lights, be overly sensitive to the feel of some clothing, textures, and react poorly to seemingly routine movements.

12. Language Processing Problems

Many children do not know how to verbally express their feelings. They may get angry with another child but cannot find the right words to use to express their frustrations. Their emotions build up and they may explode.

13. Mood Disorders

A small number of children may have bi-polar disorder or be extremely depressed and the numbers are increasing. In the August 13, 1998 *USA TODAY*, researcher Ronald Kessler from Harvard Medical School revealed that the rate of serious depression among American youth has increased from

2% in the 1960s to almost 25% in the 1990s! Many depressed children have anger outbursts.

14. Attention Deficit Disorder

ADHD appears to be primarily a biological or neurodevelopment problem. These children may have subtle abnormalities in parts of the brain that are responsible for maintaining attention, screening out distractions, and regulating motor activity. Such children get easily frustrated, are very inflexible, impulsive, and often have trouble controlling anger.

15. Sexual, Physical and Emotional Abuse

It isn't unusual for children who have been abused to have anger problems. Kenneth Dodge at Vanderbilt completed a recent study (1997) on children who were abused or maltreated by adults. He discovered that children who were maltreated were much more likely than non-maltreated children to develop a chronic pattern of bad behavior and aggression.

Roadblocks to Anger Management

In our attempts to help children with anger problems to mature, to be more flexible, and patient, we often encounter roadblocks. Here are five major ones.

Roadblock #1 Some children believe their anger is justified and appropriate.

They believe that they have a valid reason to get angry and the target of their anger is not important. They tend to blame others for their feelings and almost never feel that they did anything wrong. Many of these children show little or no empathy.

The target of their anger is not important.

Roadblock #2

According to anger expert Raymond DiGiuseppe (1995), "Anger usually occurs along the belief that the target of one's anger is a totally worthless human being. Because the transgressor responsible for the person's anger is a worthless, condemnable individual, he or she deserves the angry person's wrath and must pay for the transgression." (p. 134)

They believe they are self-righteous.

Roadblock #3

DiGiuseppe adds, "Angry people almost always believe that they have been wronged or treated unfairly. The transgressors are portrayed as morally wrong. Angry people are rarely willing to examine their own role in an interpersonal conflict." (p. 134)

Angry children often get short-term reinforcement.

Roadblock #4

Because of his/her aggressive action, the bully always gets the ball. Some students think Lisa is "cool" because she talked back to the teacher. Jimmy always gets to kick first because the other children are afraid of him. Morgan knows that if she has a temper tantrum at the store, her mother will give in and buy her a toy. Kasey may "act out" on purpose because she knows the teacher will give her treats if she starts to improve her behavior in class.

Angry children believe in aggressive cathartic expression.

Roadblock #5

Many young people feel they need to get the anger out by yelling, hitting, screaming, kicking, throwing or punching. Over the years many parents, teachers, and therapists have actually encouraged children to vent their anger by doing some of these things. While it is true that holding anger in is unhealthy—releasing it inappropriately can also be unhealthy and even dangerous.

Most everyone would agree that hitting others is not an appropriate way for children to vent anger. But what about yelling, hitting a pillow or throwing things? Research over the last fifteen years has given many mixed messages on this topic. Let's take a look at what many of the anger experts have to say on cathartic treatments.

- R. DiGiuseppe (1995) "This belief that catharsis is a corrective experience that reduces the builup of anger is false. Instead catharsis leads to temporary relief and increases the chances that one will become angry again in the future."

- Dean Hamer (1998) "The worse thing you can do, which is actually what some therapists recommend, is to "vent" yoru anger. This is a myth, and practicing it will only escalate the situation and fill you with rage." (p. 91)

- Janet N. Tyson (1998) in her book, *Common Threads of Tennage Grief,* lets grieving teens know that it is normal to get angry when they lose a loved-one. "When you feel anger, you may need to release it. Be careful not to harm property, anyone else or yourself." (p. 8). See Strategy 129 for some of her suggestions for venting anger appropriately.

- Daniel Goleman (1995) in his book *Emotional Intelligence* interviewed Diane Tice on her recent research on venting anger. Tice reported, "Ventilating anger is one of the worst ways to cool down: outbursts of rage typically pump up the emotional brain's arousal, leaving people feeling more angry, not less." (pp. 64-65)

- Carol Tavris (1984) noted, "Unhealthy ways of expressing anger can lead to miscommunication, emotional distancing, escalation of the conflict, endless rehearsals of grievances, assuming a hostile disposition, acquiring angry habits, making a bad situation worse, loss of self-esteem and a loss of respect of others." (pp. 170-191)

• P. Wendel (1997) wrote about his work with youth gangs who, when angered, sought revenge as a way of dealing with their hurt and anger. The author noted that although in gang life it is common to seek revenge for a senseless act, past gang members admit the acts of revenge only temporarily made the pain of loss go away. It didn't make it stay away and sometimes caused more grief to follow.

• And how about this one! I actually found this strategy in a 1993 publication entitled, *Practical Ideas for Counselors*. A strategy called "The Anger Punch" was written by Priebe, Rudd and Lenthall, for teachers of elementary students. Part of the article went like this, "Tell the class members that they are going to make punching bags to use when they are angry at someone. Explain that there will be four punching bags in the classroom. Whenever they are angry they should go to the punching bag that resembles the person they are angry with. The bags should resemble a girl, a boy, an adult and one for when they are angry with themselves." (p. 7) I hope this strategy is not being used in our schools!

So...what do we do? Maybe the Tibetan teacher, Chogyam Trungpa had it correct when he said this about the best way to handle anger: "Don't suppress it. But don't act on it." Here are a few "middle of the road" suggestions on the cathartic approach for children.

1. Encourage children to verbally express their concerns and anger with others.

2. Teach them prevention skills. There are several listed in Section 2 of this book.

3. Encourage children to use alternate choices to vent rather than catharsis.

4. For the small number of children who cannot suppress the anger and must let it out, provide them with appropriate avenues to vent (again, see Strategy 129 for suggestions). If possible, provide a private space for them to "let off steam."

5. Let the angry child know that when they vent they must not hurt themselves or others and that they cannot destroy property.

6. Continue to encourage them to become less dependent on always using a cathartic approach.

7. Continually help them update their conflict management skills (see The Six C's of Conflict Resolution in Strategy 32).

The 131 Creative Strategies

The following collection of strategies are grouped into four anger levels.

LEVEL 1: Mild Anger

(Strategies 1-32)

These strategies include simple reminders, preventive measures, anger management skills, classroom activities, and a few thoughts on taking a close look at ourselves and how we deal with anger.

LEVEL 2: More Challenging Anger

(Strategies 33-65)

This level provides ideas for working with the more challenging, easy-to-anger child.

LEVEL 3: Extreme Anger

(Strategies 66-108)

Strategies in this level are aimed at the extremely angry child.

LEVEL 4: When Nothing Else Works

(Strategies 109-131)

Included are emergency measures to use with children when, "Nothing else seems to help!"

15

LEVEL 1: Mild Anger

(Strategies 1-32)

Strategy 1: Don't Fuel the Fire

You cannot hope to control others until you can control your own emotions. Your job is to not only model self-control but to help calm the angry child. If you get upset, yell and scream, or threaten the out-of-control child, then you are adding fuel to the fire. Fred Jones (1987), author of *Positive Classroom Discipline*, believes that if a teacher allows himself/herself to become very upset and yell at a student, he/she will effect the situation in two ways. "First, you will generate resentment, and it is for this resentment, compounded with public humiliation, that you will pay most dearly. Second, your upset will trigger a shot of adrenaline into the student's bloodstream just as it did into your bloodstream. That adrenaline will not be out of either of your bloodstreams for approximately 28 minutes, and during that time the student will be hyperactive to external stimuli and will have a shortened attention span. When a teacher yells at a student, the student does not do much schoolwork for the remainder of the period. The reasons for this loss of learning time, Jones says, are both psychological and physiological." (p. 86)

Strategy 2: Help The Angry Child get his/her basic needs met

(Note the Skillsheet: "Glasser's Basic Needs" on page 18)

Dr. William Glasser (1984) believes that people become motivated when their basic needs are met. Besides survival (food, water, and shelter) **children need:**

LOVE	*POWER*	*FUN*	*FREEDOM*
Sense of belonging, friendship, caring, & involvement	Feeling important, recognition, skill, & competence	Pleasure, enjoyment, learning, & laughter	Choice, independence, liberty, & autonomy

Many children are not getting their basic needs met at home and then come to school and have trouble learning and behaving. The well-known blues singer, Billie Holiday said, "You've got to have something to eat and a little love in your life before you can hold still for any damn body's sermon on how to behave." Unfortunately a small number of young people take drastic measures to get their basic needs met by doing such things as turning to crime or joining street gangs. For many, a street gang gives them their love, power, fun, and freedom.

Take a few minutes to complete the skillsheet on the next page. How are you doing with your own basic needs? How well are you helping angry children meet theirs?

Glasser's "Basic Needs" Model

"I have noticed that happy people are constantly evaluating themselves and unhappy people are constantly evaluating others."

Dr. William Glasser

According to Dr. William Glasser (1998), "To understand what motivation is, it is necessary first to understand that Control Theory contends that all human beings are born with five basic needs built into their genetic structure: survival, love, power, fun and freedom. All our lives we must attempt to live in a way that will best satisfy one or more of these needs." (p. 48)

Besides survival, our basic needs are:
Love: belonging, friendship, caring, involvement
Power: importance, recognition, skill, competence
Fun: pleasure, enjoyment, learning, laughter
Freedom: choice, independence, liberty, autonomy

Take a few minutes to complete the chart below. What are you doing to meet your basic needs in your personal life? What are you presently doing to help your students meet their basic needs in your classroom? Dr. Glasser would probably agree that many children become angry if their needs aren't being met.

	What are you presently doing in you personal life to meet these needs?	List ways in which you are helping your students meet their basic needs.
Love		
Power		
Fun		
Freedom		

Strategy 3: Reframe The Angry Child's Thinking: The Six Beliefs

(Note the Skillsheet: "Six Beliefs" on page 20)

On a regular basis go over these six beliefs with the angry child. If we begin to "reframe" his/her thinking, anger problems may decrease. The Six Beliefs can be posted on the wall as a constant reminder. You may need to have your angry child review them on a regular basis.

Strategy 4: Home Court Advantage

Most basketball teams prefer to play their games on their home floor in front of their fans. They tend to feel better and play better in a familiar setting with their fans cheering them on. Let your students know that your classroom can provide that safe, comfortable "home court advantage." They may get teased and hassled in other settings but in your room everyone is encouraged to treat others kindly. Let them know from day one that you will not tolerate rudeness.

Strategy 5: Interest Inventories

(Note the Skillsheet: "Student Interest Inventory" on page 21)

During the first week of school (when most students like you and they still listen) have them fill out the Interest Inventory Skillsheet. This instrument can come in handy later in the year. For instance, if you are starting to have problems with Louis (your angry child) refer back to his inventory. You may see that he collects baseball cards. Ask him some questions about his hobby or encourage him to bring his collection to school to show others. Knowing the hobbies and interests of children can help build a bridge between you and them. The more you know about a child, and the more he/she knows about you, the better the relationship.

Six Beliefs

1. **It's OK to make mistakes.**

2. **Everyone is different and that's OK.**

3. **I can have a good day or bad day. It's up to me.**

4. **I am lovable and capable. Others are lovable and capable.**

5. **Not everybody is going to like me.**

6. **I'm learning to handle it when things go wrong.**

Student Interest Inventory

Student Name _____Date_____

When is your birthday? _____Favorite Color_____

Favorite fruit _____Favorite Candy Bar_____

Something you do well _____Favorite Soda_____

What do you Collect? _____

Your favorite restaurant _____

Your three favorite TV shows   1. _____

2. _____   3. _____

Your three favorite books 1. _____

2. _____   3. _____

Your favorite school subject   _____

What kind of music do you like? _____

Who are your favorite singers?   _____

When you are an adult, what kind of job would you like? _____

Where is your favorite place to visit? _____

What are your three most-liked table games?_____

Do you have pets?_____   What kind? _____

What are their names? _____

What other hobbies and interests do you have? _____

Strategy 6: Norm

Place a large piece of construction paper on the floor. Have a child lie on the paper and have someone else trace the outline. Cut the new person out, hang it on the wall, and name it "Norm." Have other children write a suggestion on Norm about what a "normal" class should be like. For instance, in a normal class students use good manners, say please and thank you, do not hit, etc. Throughout the year have the children refer to Norm for ideas on how to get along better with others.

Strategy 7: Hot Topics Class Meetings

Constantly monitor "triggers" that cause fights, arguments, and disagreements in class. On a weekly basis schedule class meetings to discuss the hot topics. Examples could include name-calling, talking about someone's mother in a negative way, tattling, or being bossy. At the meetings let the children sit in a circle to discuss and share concerns.

Strategy 8: Teach Them How To Give Compliments

(Note the Skillsheet: "How To Give Compliments" on page 23.)

One of the hardest things for young people to do is give others compliments. They find it easy to put others down but difficult, if not impossible, to lift others up. Give children a copy of the Skillsheet on the next page. It explains how to give compliments. Have students role play situations where they can use these. Anger problems will diminish in environments filled with kind words.

How To Give Compliments*

1. Make eye contact.

2. Speak clearly.

3. Don't speak too fast.

4. Use good timing. Some people don't want to be complimented in front of others. It may make them feel uncomfortable. Try complimenting them in private.

5. Smile.

6. Personalize your compliment. For example, instead of saying, "You are good at art," say, "I like the picture you drew in art class, especially the shade of blue you used for the sky."

7. Be sincere. The compliment must be true. No phony ones!

8. Try to pass out at least three different compliments to three different people every day.

9. Don't "over do it." If you give away too many compliments, others may think you are not sincere.

10. Whenever you receive compliments say, "Thank you."

*Adapted from Shapiro, Lawrence (1994). *Tricks of the trade.* King of Prussia, PA: Center for Applied Psychology, Inc.

Strategy 9:   Goal Setting...Miracles Come In Cans!
(Note the Skillsheet: "Miracles Come In Cans" on page 25)

Help your angry child set goals for improving his/her behaviors. Have the child complete the Skillsheet on page 25. It looks like a can and he/she must list at least five things he/she can do in order to achieve his/her goal or miracle.

Strategy 10: The Toothpaste Theory

Try this activity with children. Take out a toothbrush and some toothpaste. Squeeze some paste onto the brush then say, "I've changed my mind and I don't want to brush my teeth now." Then say, "Do you think I can get all the paste back into the tube?" The obvious answer is, "No." Then ask the children, "How is this like words we use when we are upset?" Encourage the children to be careful what they say when they get upset. Words can hurt.

Strategy 11: A Simple "I'm Sorry."

We all get frustrated at times with children and we may say something that we later regret. If we do say something hurtful to the children, take time to apologize. Children gain respect for adults who are willing to admit they made a mistake.

Strategy 12: Ignore

Yes, I still believe it is true that if we ignore some behaviors, they will stop. I remember when my son was very young he would place his hands over his ears when I was lecturing to him about his behavior. He was looking for a reaction from me. I continued my discussion and said nothing about his hands covering his ears. After a few days he ended that annoying mannerism.

Miracles Come in Cans

My goal, wish, miracle:

Strategy #9
Skillsheet

_____

To Accomplish My Miracle...

I Can _____

I Can _____

I Can _____

I Can _____

I Can _____

Student Name _____

Date _____

Strategy 13: Be Consistent

Try to be as consistent as possible with daily routines and with enforcing rules. Inflexible and easily angered children need as much consistency as possible. If we constantly change routines and procedures or if we are inconsistent dealing with class rules, then we are creating an environment that will cause the angry child to explode. Remember, be consistent or not...there is no such thing as "consistent most of the time."

Strategy 14: The "Right" Kind Of Praise

(Note the Skillsheet: "Giving The Right Kind Of Praise" on page 27)

Many years ago B.F. Skinner said that praise is " the greatest tool in behavior modification." (1993, p. 13) Over the years parents and teachers have been programmed to constantly praise children. But recent research has found that there is a wrong and right kind of praise. A new study suggests that praising children for their intelligence and accomplishments can actually damage and dishearten them, while praising them for effort helps them retain an eagerness for learning and insulates them against feelings of failure. In the July 1998 issue of *Journal of Personality*, psychologists Claudia Mueller and Carl Dweck noted that students praised for intelligence and good scores became more competitive, more likely to lie about their test results and more focused on how other children performed. All these factors increase the odds of our angry child getting upset. The researchers found that children praised for effort gravitated toward more challenging problems in school subjects and were not as concerned with other children's scores. They were more eager to learn new problem-solving strategies.

Make an effort to concentrate on praising the student's effort and not the student. For example, if your easily-frustrated student successfully handled a difficult situation on his/her own, don't say, "Jarrod, I'm so proud of you for doing the right thing." Instead say, "Jarrod, you must be proud of yourself for staying cool during that stressful event." The following Skillsheet provides more suggestions on using the right kind of praise.

Giving The Right Kind of Praise*

Children have an intrinsic desire to learn. Praise and manipulation can only serve to stifle the natural motivation and replace it with blind conformity, a mechanical work style, or open defiance toward authority.

Randy Hitz and Amy Driscoll, (1988, p. 96)

1. Don't praise people, only what they do. It's less likely that there will be a gap between what someone hears and what the child thinks about him/herself if we don't make sweeping comments about what he/she is like as a person. Saying something about what the person has done (or is doing) makes more sense: "That's a really nice story" is better than "You're such a good writer."

2. Make praise as specific as possible. Not only should we focus on the act or product, but we should do so by calling attention to the specific aspects that strike us as especially innovative or otherwise worthy of notice. Even better than "That's a nice story" is "That's neat at the end when you leave the main character a little confused about what happened to him."

3. Avoid phony praise. A parent or teacher who is genuinely delighted by or appreciative of something a child has done should feel free to let that excitement show. Remember, a four-year-old can usually tell the differences between a genuine expression of pleasure and phony praise, between a sincere smile and one that is manufactured and timed for best effect.

4. Avoid praise that sets up competition. It is never a good idea to praise someone by comparing him/her to others. Phrases like "You're the best in class" ought to be struck from our vocabulary. The research is quite clear that such comments undermine intrinsic motivation, but their most pernicious effects are subtler; they encourage a view of others as rivals rather than as potential collaborators.

5. Give positive praise in private. The older the student, the less comfortable he/she feels about getting praised in front of peers.

*Adapted from Kohn, Alfie (1993). *Punished by rewards.* Boston: Houghton Mifflin Co.

Strategy 15: I Messages

When your angry child is upset, encourage him/her to start a sentence with the word "I." This is the first step in helping the child become more responsible for his/her own feelings and actions. Once a child realizes that he/she is responsible for how he/she feels, the child can learn how to give constructive feedback to others. For example, "I feel sad when you take my crayons away."

Strategy 16: Dress Codes and Graffiti

Don't tolerate any signs of graffiti in school. Paint, wash, and get rid of anything obscene, violent, or gang-related. This establishes the mood of who's in control. Don't let it be the kids. Also, don't let your dress code get too slack. Be aware of T-shirts with obnoxious comments or advertisements or anything that might be offensive to others. Provide alternative ways for children to express themselves. For example, students could plan a dress up day at school or paint a collage together of something positive. Some schools have each grade level hallway painted differently.

Strategy 17: Thumbs Up!

Use hand signals/signs to help cue the angry child. When Sally starts to lose it, make the T-sign that athletes use to signal a time-out. This lets her know she needs to go somewhere to calm down. If Mike doesn't push or shove, give him the "Thumbs Up!" When Anthony is getting too loud, put your finger to your lips to signify, "Quiet down."

Strategy 18: Matter of Fact vs Passionate

Some adults are very passionate when it comes to discipline. They get loud, use their hands in communication, threaten, their faces get red, they lecture, and go on and on. Others are more what I refer to as "matter of fact." They stay calm, talk in a slow manner, and keeps words to a minimum. When dealing with an angry child it is important to remain calm. The more passionate you get, the angrier the child will get. Don't forget that many inflexible students have Attention Deficit Disorder which means they have trouble processing information. Being too "wordy" floods them with too many bits of information.

Strategy 19: Classroom Creatures

Animals can create a calming effect in a classroom. Even your most hostile child enjoys holding, petting and caring for a class pet. In the February 1995 issue of *Elementary School & Guidance Counseling,* authors Lucinda Trivedi and James Perl uncovered some interesting research on animals and their relationship to children.

- A 1986 study of of interviews with 20 adolescent juvenile offenders entering a residential treatment facility found that when the interviewer's dog was present the adolescents were less hostile and more apt to disclose personal information.

- Animals can be used to support relaxation training. They can model relaxation for humans because they effectively and visibly let out tension when they relax.

- A child can learn responsibility by caring for an animal.

- Research uncovers the fact that the presence of an animal can lower blood pressure in children and adults.

- Another study found that institutionalized adolescents who cared for a rabbit for six weeks demonstrated less aggressive behavior than did adolescents in alternative activity programs.

Strategy 20: "What Are You Doing?"

Many children are unaware of what they are doing. Even I have been at a faculty meeting where I started tapping a pencil on the table. The next thing I know a teacher gives me an elbow shot to the ribs and says, "Stop tapping that pencil!" I didn't realize I was tapping the pencil. Not all students misbehave on purpose. Instead of saying to a student, "Stop rocking in your chair!" try saying, "Tonya, what are you doing?"

Strategy 21: Take A Humor Break

If you sense stress building up within the classroom, blow a horn, snap your fingers, or make some silly sound. Students know that it means to put down their pencils and get ready for a joke or funny story. Laughter in the class does much to defuse a tense situation. Make sure you provide several opportunities every day for laughter. In his book, *Laffirmations,* Joel Goodman (1995) lists 1,001 ideas for bringing humor into your life everyday.

Strategy 22: Dear John

Take the time to write a personal note to the child who is struggling with anger problems. Let him/her know that you are always willing to listen and that you recognize the progress he/she is making. Put a sticker on the note that has an encouraging word that the student can remember.

Strategy 23: The Yes Theory

As often as possible, when the angry child asks to do something, say "Yes." The more you say yes the more likely he/she will accept the no. If you always say "no," after awhile he/she will stop asking and may become sneaky.

Strategy 24: Which Name Do You Prefer?

Take the time to ask the students what names they prefer to be called. My real first name is Malcolm and when I was in elementary school I had bright red hair. I hated it when teachers called me Malcolm and I would cringe when they called me "Red."

Strategy 25: Let's Play

One of the quickest ways to improve relations with an angry child is through play. Some of the biggest improvements I saw with my angry students came while playing basketball with them. Some of my best counseling sessions occurred while playing the game of Connect Four.

Strategy 26: New Games

As often as possible play non-competitive games at school. These activities, often called New Games, encourage teamwork; there are no individual winners or losers. So often I see angry children's behavior get worse after losing a ball game. Whenever I take children outside to play kickball, they must agree on my number one rule... nobody keeps score. Some examples of non-competitive games would be to have students design a machine, only using their bodies, that can move. Or a game of human knot when all students grab another student's hand and then try to unravel themselves.

Strategy 27: Organized Playtime

Research finds that most fights and arguments happen during unstructured activities (up to 60%). Think about it. Most conflicts take place in the halls, bathrooms, cafeterias, and playgrounds. I am sure you've witnessed children storming into class, upset and "fussing" because of something that happened on the playground. Often it takes several minutes to get them back on task. If you have several angry, aggressive students in your class then you may need to make playtime very structured. You may have to be the pitcher in softball and the umpire in kickball. At times you'll have to call a time-out to discuss sportsmanship, winning and losing, and taking turns. Or you can come up with some creative games/puzzles for students to do once they first come to class and before they leave.

Strategy 28: Grandma Is Right

I'm sure you've heard of Grandma's Rule. It involves a "when" and "then." "Joey, when you calm down, then you can go back and play." Have fun and teach students what the Grandma's Rule is so they will know what it means when you use it.

Strategy 29: The Block Theory
(Note the Skillsheet: "Ten Ways to Stack Your Own Blocks" on page 33.)

One of the best ways to help children control their anger is to keep them busy in positive, interesting activities and to teach them ways to enhance their own self-esteems. The Block Theory teaches young people ten things they can do themselves to feel good. I actually use a stack of wooden blocks to demonstrate. Every time a child does one of the ten things, he/she gets a block added to his/her stack. When something bad happens, the child loses a block. The goal is to have such a tall stack of blocks that the child can afford to lose one. If a child has a short stack of blocks and something bad happens (he/she gets teased or fails an exam), he/she will get angry because he/she can't afford to lose another block. I remind students not to let their stack get so high that they think they are better than others (their stack will tip over) and not to let their stack get so low that they think about hurting themselves or others. I also tell children that no one can take one of their blocks unless they allow it to happen. See the following Skillsheet for the ten ways to stack blocks.

Ten Ways To Stack Your Own Blocks

Getting along with others is not easy. Friends and classmates can say and do some hurtful things. They always try to "knock your blocks off." Even parents, teachers, and other adults do things that upset you. Instead of complaining about what others are doing to you, start doing positive things for yourself. Following are ten things you can do to stack your own blocks. Remember, the goal is to have such a tall stack of blocks that when something goes wrong (you get teased or fail an exam) you can afford to lose a block. If you have a short stack of blocks and something bad happens, you will get upset easily because you can't afford to lose a block. Every day you should say to yourself "What am I going to do today to stack my blocks?"

1. **Use the mail.** We all get excited when we get mail. Write letters to others, send away for freebies, get a pen pal, and/or subscribe to a magazine. Remember, you don't get mail unless you send mail.

2. **Read, Read, Read.** Every time you read a book, you stack a block. Reading will add more blocks to your stack rather than watching television.

3. **Do Some Work Around the House Without Being Told.** Surprise your parents and wash the dishes, mow the yard, or fold laundry. You'll feel better because you helped out and your parents will be pleased. More privileges may come your way!

4. **Diet and Exercise.** Eat good food and exercise. You'll look and feel better.

5. **Keep a Diary or Journal.** Take a few minutes at the end of each day and write down all the good, and not so good things that happened.

6. **Hobbies and Interests.** Keep busy in positive activities. When you earn a badge, score a touchdown, or get a high score in gymnastics – you stack a block!

7. **Find a Good Listener.** We all feel better when someone listens to us.

8. **Learn Something New.** One of the greatest feelings happens when we learn and/or master a new skill.

9. **Say or Do Something Nice for Others.** When you add a block to another person's stack, you actually get a block of your own. It feels good to be kind to others.

10. **Ask for a Hug.** Hugs feel great!

Strategy 30: A Hug or a Handshake?

I heard a story about a fourth grade teacher who greeted his students after lunch every day. He would ask them "What will it be, a hug or a handshake?" This teacher realized the importance of touch. We live in a society that doesn't touch enough. Many angry children are that way because they feel unloved and seldom were hugged. Don't be hesitant to shake a student's hand or place a hand on the shoulder of an upset child. A simple touch, handshake, or high five can help build a special bond between you and a child.

Strategy 31: Tell Them a Story

(Note the Skillsheet: "If Tomorrow Never Comes" on page 35)

I visit classrooms on a regular basis and I find my most successful lessons center around the numerous stories I tell. Whenever I visit a class, students ask, "Mr. Carr, are you going to tell us a story?" I have been able to gain control of some of the most challenging classes through my ability to tell stories. Children of all ages love to hear stories. Find stories that deal with anger. In the November 25, 1998 issue of *Education Week* I read an article about another counselor who loves to tell stories. Jim Woodard told of his first week on the job as a counselor at Boys Town in Nebraska. After a few encounters with particularly tough and rebellious boys, he thought his first week might be his last. But his storytelling saved him. He was able to teach valuable lessons through his powerful stories. The boys eventually called him "Jim The Storyteller."

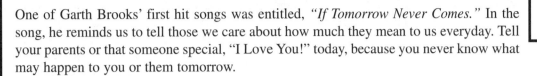

If Tomorrow Never Comes *

One of Garth Brooks' first hit songs was entitled, *"If Tomorrow Never Comes."* In the song, he reminds us to tell those we care about how much they mean to us everyday. Tell your parents or that someone special, "I Love You!" today, because you never know what may happen to you or them tomorrow.

Here is a story about a young boy who got so angry that he said and did things that he regretted later on.

Jake, who was 15-years-old, lived with his mother and his 5-year-old sister, Chrissy. Most of the time, Jake got along well with his sister. Chrissy truly loved her older brother. Since she did not know her father, she often looked up to Jake as her father. She would follow him around the house and often copy him. When he was doing his homework, she would pretend to do her math and reading. When he mowed the lawn, she was right behind him with her plastic toy mower. Jake would sit for hours in his room sorting and looking over his baseball card collection, and Chrissy would be at her little desk playing with her comic cards. The highlight of her day happened every night when Jake would read her a story before going to bed.

Jake had a terrible day at school on Monday. He failed a science test, lost his new jacket, and was accused of copying another student's homework. He was angry!

As he entered his house, he could hear some giggling and other noises coming from his room. Who was in *his* room? He pushed open his door. There was Chrissy at *his* desk with a peanut butter sandwich in one hand, and several of his valuable Nolan Ryan cards in the other. She did not realize she was doing anything wrong, she was just copying her big brother. Jake exploded, "Get out of my room this instant!" She tried to talk to him but he wouldn't listen. He added, "I Hate you, and I wish you were never born!"

Jake ignored her the rest of the evening. Several times she told him she was sorry, but he did not respond. At bedtime she cried and begged him to read her a story, but he acted like he couldn't hear her. Chrissy cried herself to sleep.

Tuesday was a much better day at school for Jake. He whistled a tune as he headed for home. On his way, he began to think about Chrissy and all the unkind things he had said to her. He told himself that as soon as he got home, he would tell her he was sorry and read her a story. As he turned into the driveway, he sensed something was wrong. His mother's car was not there and his neighbor, Mrs. Collins, met him at the door.

Jake asked, "What's wrong?" Mrs. Collins told him that Chrissy had a bad fall and his mother had to rush her to the hospital. His sister was in critical condition. Jake sat on the couch, and he remembered the last words he had said to her, "I hate you and I wish you were never born!" He thought, "What if she dies?" He prayed, "Please God, let her live."

The next ten days went by slowly as Chrissy fought for her life. Jake couldn't sleep and hardly ate any food. He promised to tell her everyday that he loved her if she came home. And she did!

* From Carr, Tom (1999). *Monday morning messages.* Chapin, SC: YouthLight, Inc.

Strategy 32: Conflict Cards

(Note the Skillsheet: "The Six C's of Conflict Resolution" on page 37)

Have your students devise a Student Belief Statement. The statement will let everyone at school know how they should be treated and how school should be free of violence. It will also encourage fellow students to resolve conflict in a positive way. Provide conflict cards for all students to carry. On one side of the card print the Student Belief Statement. On the other side list a step by step plan for resolving conflict. Students will be encouraged to refer to their cards when conflicts occur. See the following Skillsheet for a sample. It shows the Six C's of Conflict Resolution.

Concern   Is this issue really that big of a concern? Can you ignore it and move on? Some things you can learn to ignore, but if this issue/problem is a concern, then go to the next C.

Confer   When you confer with someone you ask them politely to stop whatever they are doing that bothers you. For example: "Jerry, will you please stop saying those things about my brother?" Sometimes you may want to say something nice first, "Jerrell, nice shirt man! Hey when you get home tonight, see if you can find my CD and bring it back to me at school tomorrow."

Consult   If you conferred with, say Jerrell, and he still didn't return your CD, then you need to consult with him. When you consult, you get a bit more assertive, but don't threaten. "Jerrell, I asked you to return my CD, but you didn't. Will you *please* bring it tomorrow?"

Confront   So far you tried to confer and then consult with Jerrell, but still no CD. You must confront him if this issue is still a concern. When you confront some one you ask them to meet you somewhere so the two of you can talk alone. You *don't* confront others in public. At a snack bar you say to Jerrell, "If you don't bring my CD tomorrow, then I'm calling your dad." When you confront someone, you must state a consequence. Make sure you *can* follow through with the consequence.

Combat   Combat simply means following through with the consequence. If Jerrell did not return the CD, call his dad. Keep your word. Don't feel bad. You gave him chances to return it before you took action.

Conciliate   After a day or two you may want to make an effort to restore your friend ship with Jerrell. Let him know you are not angry and let him know that you're sorry that you had to take action. Don't hold a grudge.

The Six C's of Conflict Resolution*

(for grades_____)

1. **Concern:** Is it really that big of a problem? Can I Ignore it?

2. **Confer:** Be polite and stay calm as you share your concern with the other person.

3. **Consult:** Be a bit more assertive. In private, share your concern again.

4. **Confront:** Once again, in private, share your concern using "I messages" and state a logical consequence.

5. **Combat:** If the conflict continues then you must follow through with your stated consequence.

6. **Conciliate:** Think about apologies, forgiveness, making restitution, and restoring friendships.

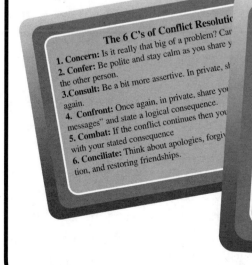

The 6 C's of Conflict Resolution
1. **Concern:** Is it really that big of a problem? Can
2. **Confer:** Be polite and stay calm as you share y the other person.
3. **Consult:** Be a bit more assertive. In private, sh again.
4. **Confront:** Once again, in private, share you messages" and state a logical consequence.
5. **Combat:** If the conflict continues then you with your stated consequence
6. **Conciliate:** Think about apologies, forgiv tion, and restoring friendships.

Student Belief Statement...

_____ *(name of school)* students believe not to fight, but to solve it right. We try to be good citizens in every way, and to work together every day. With our teachers we must respect and obey. With their guidance they'll show us the way. In order to learn, school must be safe, and _____ *(name of school)* should be such a place.

* Used with permission of the authors William Purkey & John Novak

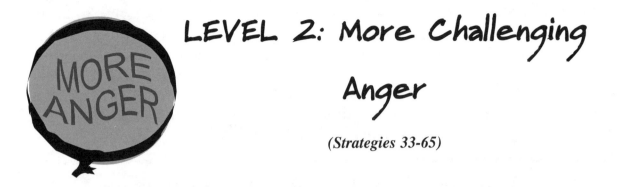

LEVEL 2: More Challenging Anger

(Strategies 33-65)

Strategy 33: Be Flexible With Orders & Give Choices

With most children you can say, "Pick those games up now and let's get to work." With the inflexible or short-fused child you may need to adjust. "Ivan, we've got work to do. Do you want to pick the games up or help me pass out papers?"

Strategy 34: Self-talk

Both teachers and students can benefit from self-talk. The teacher of a difficult student might say things to himself/herself such as, "I'm not going to let Jacob destroy my day." "When Lucinda vents her anger at me she really isn't angry at me. She's angry with her parents." "I want to say something back to her but I realize that it's better to ignore." Students can be taught to use phrases like, "I can make it through Mr. Jones' class." "It's Friday, I'll make it." "If I don't get picked for the team, I'll try again next year."

Strategy 35: A Can of STP

(Note the Skillsheet: "The STP Theory" on page 40)

This strategy can be very effective for children in grades 2-5. The famous race car driver Richard Petty used STP (oil additive) in his car to keep it "running" smooth. I tell children that sometimes they encounter problems and they need help to keep themselves running smooth. When they get upset they are told to take their STP (in their imagination). **S** means: Stay Cool. **T** means: Think Before You Act. **P** means: Practice Certain Skills. This activity teaches children ways of coping with anger and solving problems on their own. I have found STP quite successful with aggressive boys. Often I would reward a child with a token in his STP can for using his STP properly. After earning a certain number of tokens, the child could earn extra playtime.

Strategy 36: Punished by Rewards?
As often as possible, avoid tangible reinforcement.

I strongly encourage teachers to not rely too much on rewarding children with candy, small prizes, stickers, and other "bribes." Why? Because this approach is a "band-aid" measure at best. Rewarding children with tangible items may get them to behave for awhile. Once they've earned their goodies they often resort back to their old, negative behaviors. In his book, *Punished by Rewards*, Alfie Kohn (1993) notes, "A child who complies in the hope of getting a reward or avoiding punishment is not, as we sometimes say, "behaving himself."…it would be more accurate to say the reward or punishment is behaving him." (p. 96)

Throughout this book I try to provide many strategies to help the angry child. Seldom do I mention the use of tangible rewards although I will admit to using "bribes" in rare cases. Sometimes I've had to offer rewards to a select few as a way of "priming the pump" or helping them get jump-started. I try to wean these children off the tangible goodies as soon as possible.

I'll finish this topic with another Kohn quote. "What rewards and punishments do is induce compliance, and this they do very well indeed. If your objective is to get people to obey an order, to show up on time and do what they are told, then bribing and threatening them may be sensible strategies. But if your objective is to get long term quality in the workplace, to help students become careful thinkers and self-directed learners, or to support children in developing good values, then rewards, like punishments, are absolutely useless. In fact, we are beginning to see, they are worse than useless—they are actually counter-productive." (p. 162)

Strategy #35
Skillsheet

The STP Theory

Whenever you start to get upset, in your imagination take your STP.
It will help you to "stay cool."

Stay cool.

You can't solve problems when you're angry.
Count to ten, take a deep breath, or try Square Breathing.

Think of ways to handle the problem on your own.

You don't always have to tell your teacher.

Practice these steps.

1. Ignore.
2. Ask the person politely to please stop what they are doing that bothers you. (Using their first name.)
3. Move away from the person if possible.
4. Ask them again to please stop.
5. Ask an adult for help.

Stay cool
Think
Practice

One can a day
keeps you running
smooth!

Strategy 37: Why Are You Angry?

This is not a "smart" question to ask young children because most of the time they really don't know why. If you keep hounding them they may make something up just to get you to leave them alone. Older children know why they are angry but seldom share their frustrations with adults. Instead of asking, "Why are you angry?" try, "Let me know if I can help you," or "I sense that you are upset about something. I'm a good listener." With younger children constantly remind them that, "It's O.K. to be mad but it's not O.K. to be mean."

Strategy 38: Don't Play Volleyball

It takes more than one person to play volleyball. It is the same for arguing. So often an adult says something to the child then the child says something back to the adult, and the exchanges go on and on. You need to realize when it is time to stop "volleying" with the argumentative child. Know when to remove yourself from a heated exchange. Education and discipline expert Fred Jones (1987) says, "It takes one fool to back-talk, but it takes two fools to make a conversation out of it. Back-talk is a melodrama written and produced by the student. If you take your speaking part, the show goes on. If you keep your mouth shut, the show bombs." (p. 122)

Strategy 39: Square Breathing

(Note the Skillsheet: "Square Breathing" on page 42)

Over the years we've instructed angry children to take deep breaths and count to ten. You can still use that technique but here is a new one. Tell the angry child to use Square Breathing the next time. Think of a square with its four sides. This strategy involves four steps that each lasts for four seconds. Also some of you may wish to keep a bright colored picture of a square on the wall. When you see Lisa getting angry, point to the square. This will help her to remember to use Square Breathing.

Square Breathing

Before you get too angry, try Square Breathing.
There are four steps, just like a square has four sides.
Each step takes four seconds.

1 Breathe in for four seconds.

2 Hold it in for four seconds.

3 Take four seconds to let it out.

4 Pause for four more seconds before saying or doing anything.

Strategy 40:   Manipulatives

Some teachers allow the angry child to use manipulatives at his/her desk. As long as he/she isn't being noisy or distracting others, he/she may use them. The best manipulatives are those that require a little pressure to put together or pull apart. Clay is good. Yes, you may have to adjust a class rule or two for this special child. Angry kids need to keep their hands busy!

Strategy 41:   A Mellow Mint Please

During tense or stressful situations you may offer the angry child a Mello Mint®, piece of candy, chocolate, or even a stick of gum. Often the chewing motion combined with the sweet flavor/taste can help to calm the child.

Strategy 42:   Glasser's Greeting

In his book, *Choice Theory*, Dr. William Glasser (1998)brings up some interesting thoughts on how to greet children. When you greet a moody child don't ask the child how he/she is doing. The child will probably respond by saying something negative about himself/herself or others. So, instead of the often phony greeting, "How are you?," replace it with, "What are you planning to do today?" or "Anything important happening?" By doing this you are trying to get the child to "refocus" his/her thoughts away from being negative toward taking positive action.

Strategy 43:   Sandwich Approach

This idea is credited to the folks who work with difficult students at Boys Town in Nebraska. The next time you have to correct a hostile, moody child, use the Sandwich Approach. Think of a sandwich having two slices of bread and meat in the middle. The goal of this idea is to improve communication between you and that child. Here is an example: Josh is pushing another child. 1) Give him the first slice of bread by getting his attention in a positive way. "Josh, stop pushing! Thank you for stopping when I asked." 2) Now for the meat. "Josh, you could have hurt Brandon. Please be more careful the next time." 3) Now for the last slice. End on a good note. "Josh, thank you for listening and being respectful. Have a good afternoon."

Strategy 44: The Sub Club

(Note the Skillsheet: "The Sub Club" on page 45)

Write a plan with the student. Attempt to get the student to substitute (sub) one behavior for another. For example, Jennifer agrees to substitute pushing and shoving for the more acceptable "asking others politely to move." If Jennifer is successful in completing her plan/goal then she has earned a sub sandwich from the Subway Shop. (You may want to ask a local sub shop if they would participate in this incentive.)

Strategy 45: Buddy Plans

The writing of plans can be very useful and effective. These plans can be even more successful if they involve the friend or friends of the angry child. If I am working with Marcus and we decide to write a plan, I may ask him for the name of one of his friends. I invite that friend to sit with me and Marcus as we write up the plan. Both students sign the agreement. If Marcus is successful in reaching this goal, then both he and his friend share in the positive consequence. The Buddy Plans rely a lot on positive peer pressure.

The Sub Club

For teachers to give to select students

An Agreement Between: Student _____

Teacher _____

Length of Agreement: From _____ To _____

Terms of Agreement: I, _____ (student) agree to

substitute (SUB) this behavior _____

with this behavior _____.

When a student successfully completes the agreement, he/she earns a tasty sub sandwich.

Signatures: Student _____

Teacher_____

Date _____

- -

(To be completed by student at the time this agreement was made)

My favorite kind of sub is_____

I like these toppings on my sub (check the ones you want.)

___ Cheese
___ Lettuce
___ Onions
___ Tomatoes
___ Green peppers
___ Pickles
___ Mustard
___ Mayonnaise

45

Strategy 46: Be Careful With Consequences

Sometimes the angry child can get to us and we may state consequences that we later regret saying. I once told a class, "I don't want to hear a "boo" out of anyone and if I do then we are not going out!" Then one "wise guy" went "Boo!" I had to keep my word but I regretted stating the consequence because the whole class was punished for the actions of one child. Here are three points to remember regarding consequences:

• ***Don't shout consequences when you are angry.***

• ***Don't state consequences you can't keep.***

• ***Keep your word and follow through with your stated consequence.***

Strategy 47: The Pressure Point

I'm always searching for new and unique strategies to help young people control their emotions. This is one of my favorites. I explain the Pressure Point by telling them the following, true story.

"Kevin was a senior in high school. He was an excellent basketball player and often compared to stars in the NBA. Kevin had one serious problem that could have prevented him from getting a scholarship to play ball in college; he had a terrible attitude. He was quick-tempered and got thrown out of several games. He was even suspended from league play for half a season. Although he had great skills, no colleges were attempting to recruit him because of his lack of self-control. Kevin's father took him to see a sports' psychologist who taught him the Pressure Point. Kevin was instructed by the psychologist to press his thumb and middle finger firmly together for five seconds whenever he heard the referee blow the whistle. He became conditioned to the whistle. When he heard it he always pressed his thumb and middle finger together. This strategy enabled him to delay his actions by five seconds. Usually after five seconds he was not as angry and didn't say or do things that got him in trouble."

I have my students practice this tool. Once again, the purpose is to delay the child's reactions. Even a five second delay can prevent major blow-ups.

Strategy 48:   Can You Picture That?

I've had luck defusing some angry children by letting them draw. Usually the only way I ever got Brian to settle down was to give him paper and pencils and let him draw. Younger children may wish to draw pictures and tell stories about things that anger them. Try letting the child draw a picture of him/herself when he/she is angry and another picture when he/she is calm. Have him/her compare the two drawings.

Strategy 49:   "1...2...3" Magic

This discipline tool has been around for years and it still works with most children. The key is to be consistent. When Aaron is complaining, start counting slowly to three or until he stops. He knows that if you have to get to number three, there will be a negative consequence. With angry children you may want to use your fingers as a visible cue.

Strategy 50:   Red, Yellow, Green

(Note the Skillsheet: "Red-Yellow-Green Traffic Light" on page 48)

Have this tool in place for your angry child. On the floor have a red square, yellow square, and green one. When Tonya starts to get angry, direct her to stand on the red square for about three minutes to cool down. Next she moves to the yellow square to process what happened and what caused her to get upset. After two minutes she moves to the green square where she thinks of ways to deal with the problem if it occurs again.

Another way to use this method is to place a picture of a traffic light or the three colored stickers on the child's desk. When the child gets angry he/she is to place a finger on the red sticker for two or three minutes, then the yellow, etc.

RED-YELLOW-GREEN TRAFFIC LIGHT

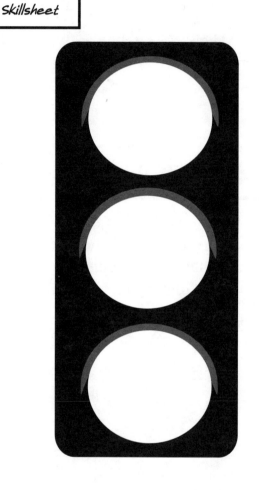

Student:

Color your traffic light. The top color is red, yellow in the middle, and green on the bottom.

Cut the traffic light out and tape it on your desk.

When you begin to get angry...

1. Place your finger on the red light for two or three minutes. Keep your finger there until the worst of your anger has left.

2. Next, put your finger on the yellow light for at least two minutes. Think about what made you angry. How did you handle yourself? Could the problem have been prevented?

3. Finally, place your finger on the green light for two minutes. Do you need to write a plan for improvement? Are you better prepared to handle the problem if it happens again? Take a deep breath before returning to work or play.

Strategy 51: Relax!

Teach the children how to relax by tightening up muscles then letting go. Play soft music in the background while they do their independent work. Let the children share ways they like to relax.

Strategy 52: Celebration Days!

Schedule surprise Celebration Days to acknowledge progress. For instance, if you notice there has been less arguing in class lately, make an announcement. "Students, I am pleased with the progress you've made in the area of getting along better with each other. Let's celebrate this achievement. Close your books, put down your pencils, and let's go outside for fifteen minutes.!"

Strategy 53: What Would MLK Do?

Many kids today are wearing WWJD bracelets. Why not let your students pick a hero or famous person and then design their own bracelets? When the angry student gets upset, he/she is to look at this bracelet for help. What would Martin Luther King Jr., Mother Teresa, or Michael Jordan do?

Strategy 54: Peace Table

Provide a special table and chairs in your room where children can go to resolve conflicts. On the peace table you may want to display flags from around the world...just like the United Nations. Encourage children to work out an agreement.

Strategy 55: Peace Tree

Designate a special tree on campus where children can visit, sit under, and talk over problems.

Strategy 56: Transition Tickets

Many angry and inflexible children have difficulties during transition time. Many of their problems take place in the halls, bathrooms, cafeteria, and playground. Keep a roll of tickets close by. Whenever your challenging child travels from one location to another without any hassles, give him/her a ticket. He/she can accumulate tickets for extra privileges.

Strategy 57: A Redirection List

At your desk always keep a list of errands. When you see Sarah getting uptight, ask her to complete one of the errands. Suggestions could include: taking articles to the office, check teacher's mailbox, stapling papers, or cleaning erasers. By redirecting Sarah's attention, you may prevent an episode.

Strategy 58: Smile!

Many angry children come from homes where their parents are unhappy, moody, and seldom laugh. These children need to see happy, warm adults in their life. Some days it may not be easy but, go ahead and smile! Just by smiling you will find your day to go by much easier.

Strategy 59: The Great Debate

Many children don't know how to debate or argue without getting angry. Provide opportunities to discuss or debate current events. Explain the rules of debating. Teach them how to listen and how to respect other people's opinions. For example, in middle school your topic could be, "Do violent movies effect the behavior of young people?"

Strategy 60: Turtles And Bears

(Note the Skillsheet: "Bears And Turtles" on page 52)

Bears and turtles react differently to stress, fear, and anger. Encourage elementary school children to think like a turtle, and not a bear, when they are upset. The following page describes this technique.

Strategy 61: Write, Tear, Stomp!

Younger children often "unwind" by writing down their problem or describing what made them angry on a piece of paper. Then they can either stomp on the paper or tear it up and throw it in the waste basket.

Strategy 62: Let's Write A Song

Most children like to write and sing songs about the importance of getting along with others. Invite a musician to sing songs with your group. Encourage your school's music teacher to use songs about peace and kindness. Have students perform their songs to the entire school.

Bears & Turtles

When you start to get angry, think of bears and turtles. If you react like a bear, you may hurt someone and get into big time trouble. If you react like a turtle, you have a better chance of avoiding a serious confrontation.

When a bear gets angry it:

1. Stands up tall

2. Shows its teeth

3. Raises its arms high

4. Sticks out its claws

5. Growls

6. Moves toward the person or another animal it is mad at

7. Has hair that stands up on the back of its neck

8. Has eyes that get big and wide open.

When a turtle gets angry it:

1. Closes its eyes

2. Pulls its head down and in

3. Pulls its arms and legs close to its body

4. Remains quiet

5. Doesn't move

6. Waits in this position until the "coast is clear"

Strategy 63: Adversity Quotient

(Note the Skillsheet: "What is Your A.Q.?" on page 54)

Explain to your children what the word "character" means. When a young person controls his/her anger and doesn't hit back is an example of someone who is developing character. Set up a corner in your room and call it the "Character Corner." At least once a week have the children circle up to hear stories about famous people who have good character. Center discussions around the topics of trust, respect, self-control, and overcoming adversities. Recognize children in your class who showed good character each week. The Skillsheet on page 54 can be used for a lesson in the character corner.

Strategy 64: You Lost What?

Educational psychologist Jerry Wilde, Ph.D. suggests using a little humor once in awhile with those children who constantly blame others for the way they feel (1996). He notes, "When students become angry, they are giving away their control, which they do not like to admit. Many students think that when they are getting angry they are demonstrating power, but in actuality, they are exhibiting weakness. There are ways of demonstrating this weakness." Here is one:

When students state, "She made me so mad," try looking around on the floor as if you had lost something. When they ask what you are looking for say, "Your control."

Student: Are you looking for something?
Adult: Yes, your control.
Student: My control?
Adult: Somehow you've lost your control over your feelings. We all have the ability to control how we feel, but somehow you've lost yours. How else could someone make you angry?

After reading this idea from Jerry's Book, *Treating Anger, Anxiety, and Depression in Children and Adolescents*, I thought of a quote by Charles H. Spurgeon, "I heard someone say that he was sorry he had lost his temper. I was uncommonly glad to hear that he had lost it, but I regretted that he had found it again so soon."

What is Your A.Q.?

(Adversity Quotient)

Everyone encounters adversities. Adversities are difficulties that people face. Here are some examples of adversities (check which ones apply to you):

❏ Having to move often
❏ Having a physical disability
❏ Not being good at math or reading
❏ Family not having a lot of money
❏ Not having transportation to go places
❏ Family involved in criminal activities
❏ Having a serious disease or illness
❏ Not having many friends
❏ Family member drinking too much alcohol
❏ Parents being too strict or too critical

❏ Have a learning disability
❏ Being too big or too small
❏ Failing a test
❏ A favorite pet dies
❏ Failing a grade
❏ Being abused or neglected
❏ Not making the team
❏ Parents divorcing
❏ Someone you love dies
❏ Not having anyone at home to help with homework

When you face adversities are you a…?

Quitter: You give up. You blame others and always use excuses.

Camper: You seldom try anything new. You won't take a risk to improve your self. You feel that others do better because they are lucky. You are pleased to get a C in math and refuse to try harder to improve your grade. You "let" things happen to you…good or bad.

Climber: You know that you are responsible for your future and for your actions. You don't blame others if you fail or make a mistake. If you fall, you get back up and try again.

* From Stoltz, P. (1997). *The Adversity Quotient*. New York: Wiley & Sons.

Strategy 65: Calming The Easily Frustrated Perfectionist

(Note the Skillsheet: "Children And Perfectionism" on page 57)

The National Association of School Psychologists published a parent/teacher handout by V. Harvey (1991) about the child who becomes a perfectionist. Following is some information from their handout.

Perfectionists try to protect themselves from embarrassment, criticism, anger, and the withdrawal of love or approval by controlling themselves and the reaction of others. Perfectionists tend to become highly anxious when they make a mistake, have a chronic fear of embarrassment or humiliation, and have self-esteem based upon perfect performance. They often have strong feelings of inadequacy and see themselves as failures due to high expectations, that they or others have of them. This results in fear of making errors or wrong decisions, desire to avoid criticism, emotional guardedness, inclination to worry, cautiousness, need to know and follow rules, and tendency to work hard. While these traits can be positive, when excessive they become rigid and result in substantial pain. They may even cause severe bouts of anger.

Children who have perfectionistic tendencies can have difficulty functioning in the classroom because their expectations for themselves are so high that completing or even attempting schoolwork is hindered. This can result in low self-esteem, chronic feelings of inadequacy, decreased performance, and increased tension and anxiety. Perfectionism has been linked to crippling performance anxiety (such as stage fright), psychosomatic disorders (such as headaches), depression, and suicidal behavior. It can emerge into an obsessive-compulsive personality disorder in adulthood.

This trait is common in gifted children and seems to result from a desire to be considered best in all situations. As a result, a gifted child may refuse to try activities rather than risk failing to achieve a superior level of performance, and consequently fall into a pattern of underachieving. Gifted children who attempt to be perfect in all aspects of their lives are also susceptible to burnout. Perfectionism can also be seen in non-gifted children. It can be particularly problematic for a learning disabled student.

Unfortunately, perfectionism has the opposite of its intended effect. Rather than saving the person from criticism and gaining love and approval, perfectionism hinders both achievement and social relationships. The following page lists ideas for helping the perfectionist.

Children And Perfectionism*

Strategy #65
Skillsheet

1. Praise effort, not just the product. For example, praise how hard a child worked on something rather than the grade achieved.

2. Refrain from over-praising: do not make what a child accomplishes more important than who he/she is as a person.

3. Mark the correct answers on papers.

4. Give permission both to yourself and the child to perform at an average level.

5. Develop realistic goals.

6. Temper tendency toward negative self-appraisal when performance did not meet unrealistic standards.

7. Discuss your own and the child's strengths and weaknesses. Emphasize that no one is superior in all areas.

8. Model and encourage graceful acceptance of your own mistakes.

9. Encourage becoming comfortable with uncertainty and ambiguity.

10. Encourage spending more time and energy learning to care about and help others.

11. Give permission to make mistakes and discuss the benefits of making mistakes.

12. Have the student sign a contract not to be perfect.

13. Have a child list the advantages and disadvantages of perfectionism.

14. Have the child keep a journal in which he/she logs in what areas of life he/she tries to be perfect, and what happens before and after instances of perfectionism.

15. Help the student explore the degree to which perfectionism affects all aspects of his/her life, including relationships, work, play, and appearance.

16. Model and encourage relaxation, meditation, listening to soothing music, etc.

17. Encourage the child to prioritize and decide which activities deserve maximum energy and which activities are less important.

18. Praise for accomplishments that have nothing to do with achievement (cooperating, sharing, and playing well together.)

19. Take gradual steps in attending social situations and joining groups.

20. Model and encourage saying, "I don't know."

*From Harvey, V. (1991). *Children and perfectionism.* Parent/Teacher Handout. National Association of School Psychologists.

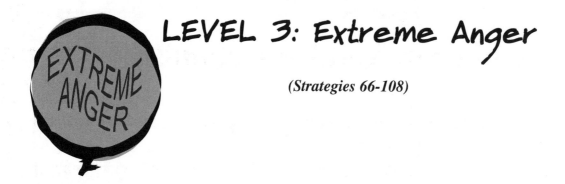

LEVEL 3: Extreme Anger

(Strategies 66-108)

Strategy 66: Sublimation

According to *Webster's New Dictionary*, the word sublimate means, "to use energy (a primitive impulse) for purpose of a high nature such as artistic creation." Angry children need positive ways to use their energy (to sublimate). Try not to take away playtime. Instead of taking all their free time, take away only five or ten minutes. Get them walking, jogging, lifting boxes, carrying books, dancing, or running errands. All these activities can reduce anger outbursts. I remember when my son was going through an anger stage. His "fits" decreased drastically during football and wrestling seasons. Those two organized sports gave him acceptable avenues for venting anger.

Strategy 67: I Get To Pick The Consequences?

Let the angry child determine the consequence of his/her misbehavior. Have it written down ahead of time. This is a step in the direction of helping him/her to become more responsible for his/her actions.

Strategy 68: Talk Lower And Lower

When encountering a loud, angry child you may have to start out talking a bit loud to get his/her attention. As you continue to talk, keep lowering your voice. The lowering of your voice often causes the child to be less noisy and it acts as a calming device.

Strategy 69: What Happened? and You May Be Right!

If you confront a very angry child, try not to blame or accuse him/her of anything at first, even if you know he/she is guilty. Some children get so angry that they only see their side of the story and may get very defensive. A good start is by asking the child, "What happened?" By asking an open question you are not blaming the child and it allows him/her to vent for a few minutes. As the child continues to talk say, "You may be right." This will also help to defuse the child. You need to let him/her tell their side of the story before you can begin to resolve issues.

Strategy 70: Empathic Assertion

This calls for the teacher to make a statement to the angry child in such a way to let the student know that the teacher is aware of the situation, and is aware of what is upsetting him/her. This lets the student know that it is okay to get angry, but it doesn't give him/her the right to disrupt class. For example, "Tim, I don't blame you for getting angry. It's okay. Erin should not have called you that name. I'll deal with her later. Now, let's get back to work." There are times when we need to let students know there is nothing wrong with getting angry. It is a normal, human emotion.

Strategy 71: Miss Bailey's Balloons

Miss Bailey always kept some balloons in her desk. She selected Roscoe as her official balloon-blower. Whenever she noticed him getting frustrated or angry, she had him blow up some balloons. If you have a student do this ask them what is needed to let some air out, such as talk about it or take deep breaths. Then have the student release some air each time they mention a strategy.

Strategy 72: Snap Out Of It!

Some easy to anger people keep a rubber band around one of their wrists. Whenever they start to get angry they are instructed to pull on the rubber band and let it gently snap their wrist. This "jolt" helps them to regain control. Note: you made need parental approval for this one.

Strategy 73: The Empty Chair

Some children need to practice expressing their anger. Julie is angry with Kisha but doesn't know how to confront her. Place an empty chair in front of Julie. Have her pretend Kisha is sitting in the empty chair. Have her practice by talking to the empty chair.

Strategy 74: Fogging

This involves using a little humor to defuse the angry child. Many children will purposely say hurtful things to get our attention. They wait for our reaction. Are we going to yell at them, send them to the office, or call their parents? The students expect the worse. Catch them off-guard and come back with a bit of humor. In the long run this may actually improve your relationship with the rude, obnoxious child. He/she gave you his/her best shot and you didn't get too upset. Instead you used humor. Use humor, but don't be sarcastic and don't humiliate. Years ago A.S. Neil wrote, "Sarcasm and humor have no connection. Humor is an affair of love, sarcasm of hate. To be sarcastic to a child is to make the child feel inferior and degraded. Only a nasty teacher or parent will ever be sarcastic." (1960, p. 361)

Strategy 75: Journals

Encourage children to write in a journal each day. Tell them to write about their feelings and have them list several good things that happened that day. There is a saying that goes, "Sometimes paper is the only thing that listens."

Strategy 76: Good Neighbors

Try your best not to isolate the angry child. He/she needs to be near some positive role models. There is a proverb that states, "Tell me who you walk with and I'll tell you what you are." If the angry child sits with other angry children, then he/she will remain an angry child. Sit him/her near some positive peers and he/she has a better chance of improving.

Strategy 77: Anger Quotes

(Note the Skillsheet: "Anger Quotes" *on page 62)*

The following page lists some of my favorite quotes on anger. Have students read them and follow up with a discussion about their meanings.

Strategy 78: Cool As a Cucumber

(Note the Skillsheet: "Cool As a Cucumber" *on page 63)*

Surprise your special child with a neat certificate. When you witness him/her staying in control during a stressful event award him/her with a certificate.

Strategy 79: Disturbing The Peace

If the child's loudness or lack of control disturbs others, you may impose a small "fine" for disturbing the peace in the classroom. This fine could be the loss of a privilege or some other consequence.

Anger Quotes

1. "He who angers you, conquers you." *Anonymous*

2. "If you are patient in one moment of anger, you will escape a hundred days of sorrow." *Chinese Proverb*

3. "Anger is temporary insanity." *Charles H. Spurgeon*

4. "Anger is one letter away from danger." *Anonymous*

5. "Anger is never without reason, but seldom a good one." *Benjamin Franklin*

6. "Speak when you are angry and you will make the best speech you will ever regret." *Ambrose Bierce*

7. "No one thinks clearly when his fists are clinched." *George Jean Nathan*

8. "Angry people typically prefer to compete rather than to cooperate."
   Dean Hamer

9. "It usually takes two people to make one of them angry." *Laurence J. Peter*

10. "You can either talk yourself into getting angrier, or you can talk yourself out of it. You have a choice. When you learn to recognize anger and work through it early on, it tends to go instead of grow." *Dr. Lenore Walker*

Cool As A Cucumber Award

COOL as A Cucumber

AWARDED TO:

_____

For staying "under control"
and handling him/herself in
a positive manner during
a stressful situation.

DATE_____

TEACHER_____

Strategy 80: Tough Skin

When dealing with the more difficult, explosive, and chronically inflexible children we need to not only be patient, but we need to have tough skin because these children will do and say some hurtful things. In his book, *The Explosive Child*, Ross Greene (1998) uses three terms that describe the actions of these more difficult children.

Vapor Lock: The stage an angry child gets into when he/she becomes totally frustrated and his/her thinking and reasoning shuts down. He/she is stuck.

Meltdown: The child loses total control of his/her thinking and behavior. He/she is beyond the point of rescue. Don't try talking with the child; he/she won't listen.

Mental Debris: During a meltdown these children are likely to lapse into their most destructive, abusive behavior. Mental debris refers to the horrible words that come out of a child's mouth during these incoherent moments.

Strategy 81: "Climbing Mad Mountain"

Dr. William Purkey from the University of North Carolina at Greensboro is credited with this term. He reminds us that many young children allow their anger to build up. Maybe they are told that they should not be angry or that it is wrong to get "mad". If they aren't allowed to let their anger out, they may explode and possibly hurt themselves or others. Purkey advises that if you sense a child's anger is building up, help him/her to find a release such as running in place, jumping up and down, or going outside to yell. Often a peace or calmness sets in after the anger is released.

Strategy 82: The Two Minute Warning

Allow angry children a short period of time to calm down. Give them opportunities to handle their frustrations on their own. Many older children get upset, refuse to cooperate, raise their voices, stomp their feet, complain, or seem to ignore the teacher. Often if you leave them alone they tend to settle down on their own. In a classroom setting, as long as they aren't hurting themselves or others, I suggest giving them about two minutes to "get their act together". If they don't settle down in two minutes then they may need to be removed from the class.

Strategy 83: Escape Passes

(Note the Skillsheet: "Escape Pass" on page 66)

All of us at one time or another has told an angry child, "Jaron, if you start to get angry, just leave the room for a few minutes." Even though we tell this to Jaron, he may still feel somewhat uncomfortable leaving the room during an important lesson. He may think that we will confront him, ("Jaron, where are you going?") or he may think that we believe he is avoiding work. A better idea is to give him three small cards (Escape Passes) on Monday morning. Tell him that whenever he needs to leave the room for a few minutes, simply place an Escape Pass on the teacher's desk...no questions asked. This gives the student a bit more control. Be sure to agree on a designated area that is safe for the student to go.

Strategy 84: The Don't Bug Me Chair

It doesn't take much to upset the inflexible, easily frustrated child. Sometimes he/she gets so wound-up that he/she needs to be left alone. In your room provide a special chair called the Don't Bug Me Chair. When a student sits in this chair no one is to talk to or bother him/her and he/she is to remain quiet. You may want to give all students in your class two or three tickets to use the chair throughout the year. You will have to set some limits on its use. Such a chair is very useful with middle school children.

Escape Passes

Escape Pass

This Escape Pass gives the holder permission to leave the classroom for up to five minutes to "cool down." Student may go to pre-approved locations only. Place this card on the teacher's desk and leave. No questions asked.

Student _____

Teacher _____

Escape Pass

This Escape Pass gives the holder permission to leave the classroom for up to five minutes to "cool down." Student may go to pre-approved locations only. Place this card on the teacher's desk and leave. No questions asked.

Student _____

Teacher _____

Escape Pass

This Escape Pass gives the holder permission to leave the classroom for up to five minutes to "cool down." Student may go to pre-approved locations only. Place this card on the teacher's desk and leave. No questions asked.

Student _____

Teacher _____

Escape Pass

This Escape Pass gives the holder permission to leave the classroom for up to five minutes to "cool down." Student may go to pre-approved locations only. Place this card on the teacher's desk and leave. No questions asked.

Student _____

Teacher _____

Escape Pass

This Escape Pass gives the holder permission to leave the classroom for up to five minutes to "cool down." Student may go to pre-approved locations only. Place this card on the teacher's desk and leave. No questions asked.

Student _____

Teacher _____

Escape Pass

This Escape Pass gives the holder permission to leave the classroom for up to five minutes to "cool down." Student may go to pre-approved locations only. Place this card on the teacher's desk and leave. No questions asked.

Student _____

Teacher _____

Strategy 85: BARK

At your desk keep a BARK (Behavioral Anger Reduction Kit). This kit should include clay, sponge balls, gum, candy, balloons, art supplies, positive affirmation cards, and other supplies designed to help angry children to regain control.

Strategy 86: Strategic Planning

This idea comes from parenting expert, John Rosemond (1999). This strategy allows you to delay the implementation of consequences. Here is and example. You notice Tiffany pushing another student. You tell her to sit down and miss ten minutes of playtime. Tiffany is so angry that she does not follow your command. She is in a "vapor lock." You know you cannot reason with her at this time. She continues to play. The following day you take your class out again for play. As you head outside you say to Tiffany, "You still owe me ten minutes from yesterday. Sit down." Strategic Planning allows you to delay a consequence and wait for an appropriate time to implement it.

Strategy 87: Getting In The Last Word

With some children it is almost impossible for you, the teacher, to get in the last word. I know for a fact that it is impossible to get the last word in with some adolescents. Even if you think you've had the last word, you probably haven't. The angry adolescent will find a way to get back at you. Also, have you ever had an adolescent stop in the middle of an argument and say to you, "Oh, I'm sorry." You are right and I'm totally wrong. I don't know what I was thinking. Please forgive me for my ignorance." No! Even if the adolescent knows you are right, he/she won't admit it. He/she will just continue to argue.

The next time you get into a heated discussion try this. Once you reach a point where you feel things are getting out of control, say this to the student, "Justin, I've said all I'm going to say. You have my permission to get in the last word. Go ahead and say what you wish." Often this catches the child by surprise and it takes all the air out of his/her balloon. Make sure you keep your word. Don't respond to his/her last word unless he/she said something disrespectful. The child may believe he/she won or has control but it isn't true. You are still in control because you granted him/her permission to get in the last word.

Strategy 88: My Hassle Log

(Note the Skillsheet: "My Hassle Log" on page 69)

Have your child keep a Hassle Log. Mark keeps a log. Whenever a hassle takes place he is instructed to check off various items, what triggered the event, how he reacted, the end result, and so on. On a regular basis sit with your student and review his/her log. Encourage the student to see what reactions caused better results.

Strategy 89: Good Behavior Book

Have students design his/her own Good Behavior Book. At the end of each day list two or three positive things that he/she accomplished in his/her book. Students are encouraged when they review these accomplishments and nice comments. Have the students share their book on a daily or weekly basis.

Strategy 90: Take A Stand

Don't stand to close to an extremely angry child. Don't "get in the face" of an aggressive adolescent! Stand to the side and talk and don't worry too much about eye contact. This posture is less threatening to an angry child.

"My Hassle" Log

Student Name_____ Date _____

1. What Happened? _____

_____

    How angry did you get?   Circle one: 0   1   2   3   4   5
                                                  0 (only a bit upset) to 5 (very, very angry)

    How well did you cope? Circle one.
             1. Didn't try to cope with anger at all
             2. Sort of tried to cope with anger, but it didn't work
             3. Tried hard to cope with anger, but it didn't work
             4. Tried hard to cope with anger, and it worked

2. What Happened? _____

_____

    How angry did you get?   Circle one 0   1   2   3   4   5
                                                  0 (only a bit upset) to 5 (very, very angry)

    How well did you cope? Circle one.
             1. Didn't try to cope with anger at all
             2. Sort of tried to cope with anger, but it didn't work
             3. Tried hard to cope with anger, but it didn't work
             4. Tried hard to cope with anger, and it worked

3. What Happened? _____

_____

    How angry did you get?   Circle one: 0   1   2   3   4   5
                                                  0 (only a bit upset) to 5 (very, very angry)

    How well did you cope? Circle one.
              1. Didn't try to cope with anger at all
              2. Sort of tried to cope with anger, but it didn't work
              3. Tried hard to cope with anger, but it didn't work
              4. Tried hard to cope with anger, and it worked

* Adapted from Bloomquist, Michael L. (1996). *Skills training for children and behavior disorders*. New York: The Guilford Press.

Strategy 91: The Eyes Say, Help!

If you ever come upon two students who are starting to fight, most of the time one of the students does not really want to fight. Once you make your presence known, look for the student who looks at you. The one who gives you eye contact is usually the one who doesn't want to battle…rescue him. If neither student looks at you, call for help immediately.

Strategy 92: Restitution

Restitution is centered around the belief that in our society today, often the victim of crime suffers more than the person who committed the aggressive act. Restitution calls for the aggressor to deal with the consequences but then make some form of restitution to the victim.

Many violent, aggressive adolescents are willing to do wrong even though they know there are consequences. In the school cafeteria Steve tells Andy that he is going to "beat up" Jerry after lunch. Andy tells Steve that if he does he'll get suspended for five days. Steve replies, "I don't care about getting suspended, I just want to get Jerry!" With restitution, Steve gets his suspension but, when he returns to school he will have to meet with Jerry and the counselor, peer mediation team or principal. Steve will have to find a way to "make it right" with Jerry.

Strategy 93: Time For A Trade

Let's admit it. There are some children that are hard to like. Have you ever had such a student? You and that student never quite hit it off. There may be times when you need to have that student removed from your class for a few minutes. Maybe the student is getting angry, arguing, or whining. This is when it is good to pair up with another teacher who is willing to accept the child for a short period of time. Make sure you return the favor someday.

Strategy 94: Back-Up Systems

Schools should have designated time-out or chill out rooms for the angry child to go when he/she needs to be removed from class. I like time-out rooms better than in-school suspension rooms. Angry children should be allowed to settle down and then get right back to class. Serving time in ISS (In School Suspension) seldom helps.

Strategy 95: A Call For Help

Have you ever noticed that if you have an explosive student in your class and he/she starts to "lose it," that if you threaten to call the office or send for the principal, the threats do not settle him/her down? In fact, some hostile students may even say, "Go ahead and buzz the office, I don't care!" These students love the attention and they feel it gives them power to act tough.

Here is an idea to get help to your class without the angry student knowing. Select a student in your class that you have developed a positive relationship with. In private tell her (for example), "Sharee, whenever I think Jason is getting too angry I will look at you and pull on my right ear lobe. This means that you are to calmly get up, leave the room, and go to the principal's office and get help."

One day Jason is ready to explode. You signal to Sharee. She leaves the room (Jason doesn't know where she's going) and in a few minutes she returns. Then, what a coincidence, who appears at the door, the principal! Now you and the principal have a secret code. If you say, "Hello Mrs. Wilson, how are you today?" This lets her know that things are under control and she can leave. But if you say, "Hello, thanks for stopping by. Why don't you come in for a few minutes and see what the students are doing?" This lets the principal know that you want her to stay a few minutes.

This strategy may be more effective then trying to send Jason to the office. Plus, it takes away some of his power. You may want to choose a different student after a few incidents so that the explosive student doesn't catch on to your strategy.

Strategy 96: Remove The Audience

In some cases you may be better off trying to remove the whole class instead of just the explosive student. By sending your class out into the hall you accomplish two things: 1, your students will be safe, and 2, by removing the audience your explosive student may not put on such a big show. When no one is watching, the angry student tends to settle down quicker.

Strategy 97: Everybody Needs An Ally

Try to support your angry child whenever he/she needs help. Let him/her know that you are always there. Also, one of the best ways to build a closer relationship with this child is to ask him/her questions about topics that he/she has an interest. For example, "Cindy how do you shut off this computer?' or "How much do you think this Tom Seaver baseball card is worth?"

Strategy 98: Desensitization

This involves exposing (a little at a time) the angry child to events or situations that often trigger episodes. If Michael always gets uptight in music class, try the following. For a visit or two you may go to class and sit with him. Next, have him go on his own for the first ten minutes of class. The next visit he tries for 20 minutes. Your goal is to help Michael to eventually make it through the whole period.

Strategy 99: Teacher Selection

I don't believe that extremely angry children should be randomly placed in classes. At the beginning of the year the principal and counselor need to take a close look at placing these challenging children. Some teaching styles and classroom environments can prevent many problems. If you place an angry, inflexible, child in a class where the teacher is loud, passionate, and impatient, then you are creating a bad situation.

Strategy 100: Time As A Consequence

If Kim's outburst caused the teacher to lose ten minutes of teaching time, how is she going to make it up? How is Kim going to make it up? Could her disruption cost her ten minutes of volleyball practice after school? Joey's behavior caused his mom to get thirty minutes behind schedule. Should he go to bed thirty minutes earlier that night? Time as a consequence can be very effective.

Strategy 101: Check Your Records

You may need to keep a notepad handy to record Garrett's actions. How often does he get upset? What triggered the outbursts? Your notes may be very useful later on as you seek help for him. Be sure to keep these notes where students cannot see them.

Strategy 102: Assertiveness Training

Invite the school counselor, social worker, or school psychologist to your class to do lessons on assertiveness. Young people need to learn how to be assertive without being aggressive. Have students role play situations where they can practice being assertive.

Strategy 103: Keep Him/Her On Your Radar Screen

With some of your more aggressive and inflexible students, you must constantly monitor their whereabouts. Don't forget, most serious behavior problems occur during unstructured times. Keep a close eye on Jermaine when he travels the halls or heads out to the playground. Don't let him get off your radar screen! If you can't see him he may be getting into a situation where he'll get into trouble. By keeping him on your radar screen you may be able to prevent many problems.

Strategy 104: "Your Passport, Please"

Design a realistic passport for Angry Amy. Include her picture, vital information (i.e., telephone number, address, and homeroom teacher). She carries the passport with her to all classes. If she behaves well and stays "cool" in those others classes, then the teachers "stamp" her passport. She can accumulate "stamps" and earn privileges.

Strategy 105: Givin' It, Takin' It, Workin' It

This idea comes from a violence prevention program. The goal is to teach children how to take criticism, how to listen, and how to compromise. Simple old arguing never accomplishes anything. Thomas Jefferson said, "I never saw an instance of one or two disputants convincing the other by argument."

Givin' It: calmly and respectfully expressing criticism, disappointment, anger, or displeasure

Takin' It: listening, understanding, reflecting, empathizing, and appropriately reacting to criticism and the anger of others

Workin' It: identifying the problems and possible solutions, suggesting alternatives when disagreements persist, and learning to compromise

Children are to be presented with this outline. Then they are encouraged to rehearse and role-play.

Strategy 106: Levels

Develop a "levels program" with the angry child. Have him/her on a system that has levels ranging from 0-5. Depending on his/her behavior and self-control he/she will move up or down levels. Every day let the child know which level he/she is on. The better his/her behavior, the higher the level. If his/her behavior is poor (hitting, pushing, having tantrums, etc.) then he/she drops to a lower level. The higher the level, the more privileges the child receives. If he/she drops to a level below 3 then he/she may lose some of the basic classroom privileges.

Strategy 107: Cognitive Restructuring & Behavior Skills Training

Refer your angry children for counseling that involves cognitive restructuring and behavior skills training. Cognitive Restructuring involves helping the angry child question the evidence, examine options and alternatives, how to decatastrophize, look at the advantages and disadvantages of his/her actions, how to turn adversity to advantage or challenge, and learn cognitive rehearsal (Reeder, 1991). Behavioral Skills Training involves targeting five clusters of behaviors: cooperation, assertion, responsibilities, empathy, and self-control (Morrison & Sandowicz, 1994). Check to see if the school counselor, social worker or mental health counselor has a group where students learn these skills.

Strategy 108: Soda Pop Pressure Release

(Note the Skillsheet: "Soda Pop Pressure Release" on page 76)

Think of your explosive child and compare him/her to a bottle of soda. If you shake a bottle of soda, fizz and pressure will build up. If you open the bottle quickly, you'll have a big mess to clean up. If you release a little pressure at a time then the fizz will settle down. With your child you can see the pressure building up. Throughout the day you will need to provide activities and opportunities to release some of the pressure so it doesn't increase to a point where he/she will explode. Once an hour you may have him/her jog in place, do some exercises, stack books, take deep breaths, etc. Remember, release a little pressure at a time and you'll prevent bigger problems.

Strategy #108
Skillsheet

Soda Pop Pressure Release

Student/Child Name_____

List Scheduled Daily Times and Pressure Release Activities.

Time	Activity
9:15	*Jog in place for two minutes*
	(example)
_____	_____
_____	_____
_____	_____
_____	_____
_____	_____

Remember, don't let the child's anger build up like pressure can build in a soda bottle. Plan to help the child release a bit of pressure on a regular basis to avoid a big pressure/anger release.

LEVEL 4: When Nothing Else Works

(Strategies 109-130)

Strategy 109: The Referral

If you've reached a point where things are getting worse with your angry child, then you and other professionals need to discuss a referral. Does the child need help from the school counselor or is outside family counseling necessary? Is the child's pediatrician involved? Does the school need to do educational testing and complete a psychological test? Does the child have a learning disability? Is he/she depressed? Does the child have ADHD, Conduct Disorder, or Oppositional Defiant Disorder? See the Appendices A, B, and C for criteria on these disorders.

Strategy 110: Remember, There Are No Quick Fixes

Just as it is impossible to improve a child's reading level by three grades in three tutoring sessions, don't expect great improvement in Jenny's behavior after three counseling sessions! We all need to be patient. I often tell teachers that some years the best they can do is to keep the angry child from getting worse. If the child doesn't regress, then that's progress! I also remind teachers and parents that there will be times when they won't be able to do much to make the child "get better" but there is much they can do to make things worse. It is important to notice only improvement no matter how small.

Strategy 111: Hands Off!

(Note the Skillsheet: "To Restrain Or Not To Restrain" on page 79)

Try to never grab, hold, or restrain an angry child unless he/she is hurting themselves or others.

Strategy 112: A Tantrum-Free Time

For every two-hour block that third-grader Kevin doesn't have a tantrum, the whole class gets a treat. Let Kevin pass out the treats.

Strategy 113: Bring in the Troops!

If you have several angry, inflexible students in your class then you need to be creative and come up with ways to spread them out. Negative attitudes and behaviors feed on each other. Here is a story of how one teacher survived a year with several angry students.

After the first week of school John realized he had a long year ahead of him. His fifth grade class was full of challenging personalities. The students could not get along. He tried several strategies but nothing worked. The students argued, fought, tattled, and couldn't work in groups. John realized that the only way his students were going to learn much that year was to spread them out as often as possible.

John spent several hours on the phone-recruiting volunteers from the community. He found three or four reliable parent volunteers. He sought help from several of the county's support personnel. He got very creative with his daily schedule. With his revised schedule and all his help, his whole class of students were together as a group for less than an hour a day. Parent volunteers took small groups to the media center for reading, mentors worked with students in the computer lab, the counselor took small groups for social skills training, and a retired physical education teacher took students outside to play. John ended up being more of a coordinator than a teacher that year but, the students learned a lot, and he survived!

To Restrain Or
Not To Restrain?

"Don't move a child roughly if you can move her gently; don't move her gently if you can tell her to move; don't tell her if you can ask her."
Alfie Kohn

1. Check with your principal. What is the school's policy on restraining children?

2. Invite your county's Director of Exceptional Children to lead a workshop at your school to go over acceptable strategies for handling extremely violent, aggressive children.

3. If a student refuses to leave the room, call the office. Don't physically force the child.

4. If a child runs out of the class or runs away from you, don't chase. Call for help.

5. Use physical restraint for safety issues only. Is the child hurting himself/herself or others?

6. If for some reason you do have to hold or restrain a child, have another adult present as a witness.

7. Don't restrain for compliance.

8. Don't restrain if you are angry.

9. Document the event.

10. After the event, talk out your feelings with a co-worker.

Strategy 114: A Pro-social Classroom

Some years a teacher may have a very challenging group of students who are easily angered, lack social skills, and cannot seem to get along. The teacher may have to focus more on social skills than academic skills. Until the students learn how to behave and get along, little learning will take place. Plan the beginning of each school year to do fun activities where students learn about each other and how to work together. According to Marion (1994) "Adults create the emotional climate in which other social, interpersonal behaviors occur. Concern for others develops in an emotional climate in which children have access to all their emotions, including anger." (p. 158)

Strategy 115: Dominos®

With some children you may have to try an incentive program to get them "jump-started." One such program involves Dominos®. Dump a box of Dominos® into a large hat. Every time John goes a certain period of time without any major problems, let him reach into the hat and pull out a Domino®. The number of dots on the Domino® will count as points on his way to earning special privileges. Most students enjoy this activity because they never know how many dots or points they will earn at a time. John may pull out three "sixes" in one day…18 points. On another day he may pull out three Dominos® with only one dot for a total of only three points for the day.

Strategy 116: Pilot to Co-Pilot

Coordinate a Co-Piloting™ mentor program with your counselor and community volunteers. A one to one relationship with a Co-Pilot™ mentor can have a positive impact in a child's life.

Strategy 117: Inform Others

As Ross Greene (1998) notes, "All adults who interact with the angry child must have a clear understanding of unique difficulties, including specific factors that fuel his/her episodes." (p. 20-23) Be sure to tell the art teacher, the baby-sitter, the little league baseball coach, the substitute teacher and anyone else who has to have dealings with Louis, about certain situations that may trigger an anger outburst. These adults need a list of Do's and Dont's on how to interact with Louis.

Strategy 118: A Bit Of Confusion

After Terry pitches his "fit" say something like this to him. "Terry, you sure were angry but at least you didn't hit anyone and you didn't break anything." This often confuses the child. The point of this strategy is to let the child know that yes, he did do wrong when he had a tantrum, but it could have been worse. For some kids, this is progress. They yelled and screamed but didn't destroy things.

Strategy 119: Eliminate Frustrations

I once had a third grader who hated to go to music class. Whenever he did, he had an episode and some episodes were so severe that he had to be suspended from school. After trying several strategies within the music room that didn't help, I decided to remove this frustration (music class) from his schedule for awhile. Sure, he missed music, but his episodes decreased, he wasn't suspended, and his overall behavior improved. My goal was to eventually get him back in music once I felt he was better prepared to handle the frustrations.

Strategy 120: Update Your Files

(Note the Skillsheet: "Files, Files, Files" on page 83)

With the extremely angry child you may want to get a file system set up. Label them "File A", "File B", and"File C".

In File A: Place a list of behaviors that take priority with this child. These behaviors will usually revolve around safety issues. You can't let your angry child hurt himself/herself or others. In this file you should have only two or three behaviors that you will focus on. You will not ignore these behaviors.

In File B: Place a list of important behaviors that you want the child to accomplish but in the beginning these behaviors are not a priority. For example, you may put "no swearing" in File B. This is important but not as important as safety issues. You may have to ignore some of the "bad words." Eventually you hope to put "no swearing" in File A. This file again, should not have too many rules/behaviors listed.

In File C: Place those "minor misbehaviors" that you are willing to ignore for now. Remember, with the extremely angry child you'll be better off ignoring minor misbehaviors and focusing on safety issues.

Strategy 121: Individual Schedules

I know of some schools that have made arrangements for angry students to go to school for half a day only. They do all their major subjects and lessons in the morning then leave around 11:30am. Other students go to several different teachers throughout the day instead of staying with just one teacher. This helps the homeroom teacher so he/she does not have to have the angry student more than an hour a day. Some schools provide evening classes in which students get their lessons in smaller classes in a short period of time (i.e., 6-8pm).

Files, Files, Files

With extremely explosive, inflexible children you need to prioritize their behaviors. Until they mature and become better able to cope with frustrations, you'll have to focus on safety issues first and ignore other (less important) behaviors. See strategy #120 for a more detailed description.

Child's Name _____

Place only 2 or 3 behaviors in this file. Safety issues only.

List a few important behaviors that you may have to ignore for awhile. Your goal is to eventually get these in File A.

These are minor misbehaviors that you may need to completely ignore while you focus on File A.

_____

_____   _____   _____

_____   _____   _____

                       _____   _____

                                              _____

                                              _____

Strategy 122: Big Brother/Big Sister

Many older students make excellent mentors to younger students who need help controlling their anger. Once they are seen as a role model their behavior improves as well as their little brother or sister.

Strategy 123: A Crisis Team

If you're not already involved with a Crisis Management team, get involved. Sometimes it takes a collaborative effort of many professionals to decide on the best approach for a child. Remember, the African saying, "It takes a village to raise a child."

Strategy 124: Shadowing

If the child is unmanageable and the parents/guardians want him/her to be in school then one idea is to have one of the parents/guardians shadow the child. This involves having the parent/guardian be with the child all day long. Many angry children improve quickly after a few days of shadowing!

Strategy 125: Pedal Pushing Power

This one may seem "unusual or extreme" but it can be very effective. Keep a stationary bicycle in the back of the classroom. Let Jennifer ride the bike for five minutes several times throughout the day. You'll be surprised at how this strategy reduces anger outbursts.

Strategy 126: Cartography: Map Making 101

When children reach the upper grades of elementary school or enter middle school they gain more independence and oftentimes find themselves without constant adult supervision like they had during their primary grades. In a recent study completed by the University of Michigan (*Education Week*, June 23, 1999) researchers had students look at maps of their schools to determine where violence occurred. Of all the acts of violence reported, most took place in locations where few or no adults were present. About 40% of the incidents took place in hallways between class periods. Another 20% happened in cafeterias during lunch time. Other problem areas were gyms, auditoriums and parking lots.

Meet with your more angry, inflexible, easily-frustrated students. Have them draw a map of their school. Let them point out areas of their school where most of their angry behavior problems take place. By utilizing their maps they can learn new avenues to travel that will allow them to avoid potential problems and conflicts.

Strategy 127: Teach "Emotion Talk"

Marian Marion (1994) suggests that teachers use a strategy known as "Emotion Talk" with older, more aggressive students. The goal of this strategy is to get the student to use the proper terms for anger and to understand the meaning of each of the terms. Examples include: "I was annoyed by her actions." "I was angry because Sheila didn't return my pencil." "I was enraged when he glared at me!" The idea is to have students properly label their feelings. In other words, not all levels of anger are the same. Annoyed and enraged are quite different.

Strategy 128: Public Resource Officers

Young people who do not learn how to control their anger often become adults who get into trouble with the law. Because of this fact many middle and high schools in our country have hired police officers or public resource officers to be present on campus. One of the main goals of this program is to help form a more positive relationship between students and the police. These officers roam the halls and mingle with students. They carry on informal meetings, eat lunch with students, play ball and teach classes on topics such as bullying or handling conflict. If your county has such a program, take advantage of it. Have an officer meet with your angry student once in awhile. The officer can become a friend, mentor and advocate for the child and hopefully the child will not look at the police in a negative manner.

Strategy 129 "I Can't Hold It In Any Longer!"

We must do all we can to help a child vent his/her anger in acceptable/safe ways. Occasionally you will find a child who tells you that he/she can't control his/her anger any longer or that he/she is about to explode. Author and counselor Janet N. Tyson encourages young people to try some of the following ideas to release anger:

☞ Tear old newspapers or magazines into shreds and throw away.

☞ Yell in the shower or with loud music playing.

☞ Throw a basketball at a hoop.

☞ Hit a tennis ball on a backboard.

☞ Throw a sponge in the shower.

☞ Do chores that require large amounts of energy like mopping, mowing or raking leaves.

☞ Hit a mattress or pillow.

Strategy 130:   Never Wave the White Flag!

We must never give up on these children. They can take up a lot of our time and energy; they can drain us, both physically and emotionally. With love, kindness, understanding and patience most angry young children can become successful adults. But we must also be honest with ourselves. There may come a time when we've done all we can and more extreme measures may become necessary. A very small number of these children may not be able to cope with school and they may need to be sent to a residential facility. This may sound horrible but there are numerous facilities in our country that do wonders for these needy children. Consult with the school's counselor, social worker or psychologist.

Strategy 131:   Tips for Parents of an Angry Child

(Note the Skillsheet: "How Do You 'REACT' To An Angry Child" *on page 88)*

In order to truly help the angry child, it is crucial that the school and family work closely together. Teachers, counselors, principals and other support personnel should always be available to provide support for the often-frustrated parents. Besides being good listeners, the school staff should provide parenting classes, create parent resource rooms, and help coordinate outside of school referrals.

This section of the book includes my "REACT" approach for helping parents who have children with anger problems. It is a simple, yet practical tool that outlines ideas to help parents react to their angry child in a positive manner. As mentioned earlier in the book, there are times when adults may not be able to do much to help the angry child improve, but there are many things that adults can do to make things worse. Many strategies presented in Section 2 can be shared with parents, but this strategy is written specifically for parents and it is in a format that allows you to make individual copies for parents and can be used as a guide for a five-session parent workshop. See the following skillsheet of "REACT."

How Do You *"REACT"* To An Angry Child?

Strategy #131
Skillsheet

How parents react to their children's anger is crucial. Adults can help defuse the anger, or they can make it worse. An important finding of the George Washington University study, is that negative parents, have a statistically stronger effect-causing bad behavior-than positive parenting has in causing good behavior. Occasionally blowing up at a child, or even a well-deserved spanking, is not going to do permanent damage. The danger is slipping into negative habits, into a pattern of negative behavior toward the child, because bad parenting is what has the strongest impact.

The next time you encounter an angry child, be careful how you <u>REACT!</u>

Remove the guilt or blame. You may not be the cause of the child's anger. You, as the teacher or parent, may be doing the best you can. Even good parents can have a difficult child. The child may have been born with a genetic tendency toward a temperament that is more moody, irritable, or short fused.

Educate yourself. Have you learned strategies to deal with the angry child? Are you up to date on the latest research on children with ADHD, ODD, or CD? Do you use self-talk? Are you taking good care of yourself (diet, exercise, rest, etc.), that helps you cope better with stress? Do you know when to stop arguing and/or remove yourself? Are you good at recognizing anger cues?

Acknowledge/Accept the fact that your child or your angry student has a difficult temperament/personality. Once you accept this fact, then do the best you can to help the angry child adjust/cope with his/her emotions.

Coach, Cheerlead, and Counsel the angry child. Many angry students do not go willingly to anger management classes, but they react well to shorter exchanges of suggestions, ideas, and praise.

Territory Check. Monitor the child's anger outburst, fights, and tantrums. Where are they happening? Where is the territory? Does it always happen with his/her sitter, at school, or in his/her neighborhood after school? Children placed in good territories have fewer anger problems. Keep them busy in sports, church, scouts, 4-H, etc.

HOW DO YOU "REACT" TO AN ANGRY CHILD?

How parents react to a child's anger is very important. They can either help to defuse the anger or they can actually do things to make the situation worse. The next time you encounter your angry child, be careful how you react.

Remove the Guilt or Blame

1. Before you can begin to help your child you must remove all guilt or blame. Yes, you may have made some mistakes along the way but you can't go back and change things that happened in the past. Forgive yourself and move on.

2. You may be doing the best you can. Even the best of parents can end up with a difficult child.

3. Always remember David Rowe's quote. When it comes to children's personalities and behaviors, "Parents should take less blame when things go wrong with a child and claim less credit when things go well." (1990, p. 611)

4. Don't let others put all the blame on you. Over the years teachers, therapists, and other professionals have been guilty of placing too much blame on parents. William Wright (1998) wrote about this in his book, *Born That Way*. He noted, "The new genetic perception has a potential for dispelling guilt on both the part of those with behavioral problems and on the part of parents who, in the environmental paradigm, have been wrongly accused of causing it. One's heart goes out to the couple who stares at the floor as a therapist explains that their lack of love and support for their son has turned him into a depressed addict they now confront. Often they are too cowed by the degree-holder before them and too ashamed of their inevitable parenting failings to cite less supportive parents whose kids turned out okay." (p. 5)

5. More and more research is finding that personality traits are influenced about 50% by genetic factors and 50% by environmental factors.

6. Certain disorders can be inherited (i.e., ADHD, depression, bi-polar disorder, and others).

7. Don't try to be a Super Parent. Strive to be a Good Enough Parent.

Educate Yourself

1. Take care of yourself. Get rest, exercise, eat well, have hobbies and interests, and laugh. You need emotional escapes from your challenging child.

2. Continue to provide your child with unconditional love. He/she still needs hugs, kisses, and your patience.

3. If your child has ADHD, Oppositional Defiant Disorder, a learning disability, or other factors leading him/her to have trouble controlling his/her anger, you need to do your homework. Read books, seek advice from professionals, attend workshops, and join a support group.

4. When dealing with the angry child, try to stay away from "severe" punishments, such as long term consequences and spankings. Much research finds that harsh punishment can actually cause some children to become even angrier. Leonard Eron, a research psychologist at the University of Illinois, studied 870 eight-year-olds in rural New York (1994). He studied how severely they were punished. His indicators ranged from no physical punishment at all to slaps and spankings. He then asked other children to judge how aggressive the children in the sample were. The more aggressively children were punished, the more aggressive they were with other children. Twenty years later, Eron again studied the aggressive children as adults. It was no surprise that they had become aggressive adults with aggressive children.

In their book, *The Authoritarian Personality,* Adorno, Frenkel-Brunswik, Levinson, and Sanford describe a type of parenting known as "authoritarian" which describes a parent who is very strict and very demanding. Children raised with such harsh and unreasonable discipline dare not direct their anger and frustration at the disciplining parents, who have the power to hurt them further. Instead, the children's anger and frustration is directed at people outside the home (i.e., teachers, peers, and others).

5. Here are some "Quick Tips" to use at home with your angry child.

   ✔ Look for cues that trigger explosions. Be able to redirect his/her attention when he/she gets frustrated.

   ✔ Don't try to reason with an angry child. Stay calm. Don't add fuel to the fire by yelling, screaming, or threatening.

   ✔ With an explosive child you may have to ignore several small misbehaviors and focus on only two or three major behaviors.

   ✔ Role model healthy conflict resolution skills. Show your child that you can control your anger.

   ✔ Use a "matter of fact" approach instead of the passionate approach to parenting. If you get too "wordy" you may bring out even more anger.

   ✔ Pick your battles. Ask yourself, "Is this really that big of an issue?"

   ✔ Send yourself to time-out. Sometimes you might be better off removing yourself from a stressful situation. This may be more effective than sending the child to his/her room.

   ✔ Don't argue. Say what you need to say, state the consequence, and walk away.

   ✔ Keep them busy. Children need to be involved in out-of-home activities such as sports, clubs, scouts, and church where they are busy and not bored. They learn more social skills, feel good about themselves, burn off energy, and tend not to get angry as often as "non-involved" children.

6. There may come a time when you need to seek counseling before things get too far out of control. See page 94 for an excellent example of how involved and helpful a counselor, psychologist, or therapist can be.

Acknowledge/Accept the Fact That Your Child Has A Difficult Temperament

1. Once you can accept this fact then you can begin to do your best to help the child adjust and cope with his/her emotions. Most angry children do mature and learn how to live with their difficult, somewhat challenging, temperaments, Unfortunately some may never learn how to "totally" control their anger but with love and support we can help.

2. When children learn how to overcome negative aspects of their personalities or temperaments, they are building character. For instance, when Larry learns not to hit others when he is angry, he is showing character. If Lillie has a very impulsive personality and eventually learns how to control her impulses, then she is showing character. Help your child develop good character. Yes, your son/daughter may be short-fused and inflexible, you can accept that fact, but he/she needs to know ways to overcome these negative characteristics. You can not let him/her use the "not so good" aspects of his/her temperaments as an excuse for their actions.

3. When trying to understand, acknowledge or even accept your child's difficult temperaments think of Harvard professor Jerome Kagan's rather interesting theory. He noted, "The brains of a million people are like a million different cans of tomato soup, each having a slightly different combination of rosemary, pepper, salt, and thyme. Each particular brain profile influences mood affect, and behavior. Of course, many different temperaments will be common, but there will be some rare temperaments. Although a child is born with a temperamental bias, the environment soon begins to act on it." (1998, p. 55)

Coach, Cheerlead, and Counsel

1. Most angry children will not sit through long lectures by parents. They may roll their eyes, put their hands over their ears, turn away, or want to argue. Keep your messages short and to the point. You don't need a twenty-minute speech to let Larry know it is wrong to hit others. Probably the most effective way to approach/address the angry child is by using the 3 C's: coaching, cheerleading, and counseling.

2. *Coach:* At the start of every day or whenever the child has to face a difficult situation, try saying things like, "You can do it!", "Remember, don't allow Jessica to make you lose your cool." "If she starts calling you names, just smile and walk away." Coaching involves giving the child advice and encouragement in small doses.

3. *Cheerlead:* "Hey, way to go David!" "What a great job of staying cool. You must be proud of yourself." "No matter what others say, we think you're great!" "Let's celebrate your progress of avoiding sticky situations."

4. *Counsel:* What I am referring to here is finding the time for just you and your child to carry out a pleasant conversation to discuss important issues. Use good thinking and make sure the conversation is "two-way." This may mean talking at midnight while the both of you are watching a movie and eating pizza. Try talking while playing a table game.

Territory Check

1. A very important role of parents is to place their children in good territories. Children need to be around positive peers.

2. Encourage, invite, and support them in activities such as sports, church, scouts, clubs, music and other interests.

3. Beware of the hours of 3-6pm. This is the time of day when most children begin to get involved in risky behaviors such as smoking, drinking, drugs, and sex. Where are your children at that time of day? Is their territory, hanging around negative peers in the neighborhood or the football field, volleyball court, or the band room at school?

4. The older children get, the less time they want to spend at home. Parents must do all they can to "navigate" them toward good peers in good territories.

5. Territory checks also involve keeping notes of the locations where the child is having the most outbursts. Does he/she have episodes on the bus, in after school care, when he/she is with his/her brother, or when playing ball? At times you may need to help the child avoid certain territories until he/she is better prepared to deal with them.

Other Tips for Parents

In the March/April 1998 issue of *The Family Therapy Networker*, authors Efran, Mitchell, and Gordon describe a challenging eight-year-old boy named Brian. He was very aggressive and violent. He was referred for therapy by his single-parent mother. While the boy received counseling, help was suggested for the mother. The following are some strategies suggested to the mother to ease a stressful home environment:

1. The mother was encouraged to change her work shift so that she would be less tired and more available when Brian came home from school.

2. A staff member gave her a quick, down-to-earth course in anger management, including methods of discipline appropriate for a reactive, aggressive youngster.

3. The mother was taught to avoid lecturing Brian during tantrums. Instead, she was to repeatedly verbalize her understanding of his frustration, while helping insure his physical safety.

4. When there were signs that he was starting to lose control, she was to move closer to him, administering a dose of "antiseptic affection" by means of a gentle touch or a non-judgmental comment.

5. Whenever possible, the mother was to express her own frustrations in "I" statements, rather than moralizing or engaging in character assassination.

6. If Brian was about to destroy property in anger, she could "set the limit" and simultaneously provide a socially acceptable alternative mode of expression: "Chairs are not for throwing. Show me on a pillow what you'd like to do to him."

7. She was to keep rules to a minimum, set consequences in proportion to transgressions, and whenever possible, convert mandates into chores.

8. Baby-sitting arrangements were made so the mother could have some time to herself to shop, exercise, or relax.

9. Arrangements were made to get Brian involved in sports such as football, soccer, and baseball. These sports gave him appropriate avenues to release or "burn off" his anger.

Appendix A:

Criteria For Attention Deficit/Hyperactivity Disorder

The patient has either inattention or hyperactivity-impulsivity (or both), persisting for at least six months to a degree that is maladaptive and immature, as shown by the following:

Inattention. At least six of the following *often* apply:

✔ Fails to pay close attention to details or makes careless errors in schoolwork, or other activities

✔ Has trouble keeping attention on tasks or play

✔ Doesn't appear to listen when being told something

✔ Neither follows through on instructions nor completes chores, schoolwork, or jobs (not because of oppositional behavior or failure to understand)

✔ Has trouble organizing activities and tasks

✔ Dislikes or avoids tasks that involve sustained mental effort (homework, school work)

✔ Loses materials needed for activities (assignments, books, pencils, tools, toys)

✔ Is easily distracted by external stimuli

✔ Is forgetful

Hyperactivity-Impulsivity. At least six of the following *often* apply:

Hyperactivity

✔ Squirms in seats or fidgets

✔ Inappropriately leaves seat

✔ Inappropriately runs or climbs (in adolescents or adults, this may be only a subjective feeling of restlessness)

✔ Has trouble quietly playing or engaging in leisure activities

✔ Appears driven or "on the go"

✔ Talks excessively

Impulsivity

✔ Answers questions before they have been completely asked

✔ Has trouble awaiting turns

✔ Interrupts or intrudes on others

- Some of the symptoms above began before age seven.
- Symptoms are present in at least two types of situations, at school, work, home.
- The disorder impairs school, social, or occupational functioning
- The symptoms do not occur solely during a pervasive developmental disorder or any psychotic disorder, including schizophrenia.
- The symptoms are not explained better by a mood, anxiety, dissociative, or personality disorder.

From American Psychiatric Association (1994). *Diagnostic and statistical manual of mental disorders, fourth edition.* Washington, DC. (pp. 83-84)

Appendix B:

Criteria For Conduct Disorder

For 12 months or more, the patient has repeatedly violated rules, age-appropriate societal norms, or the rights of others. This is shown by three or more of the following, at least one of which has occurred in the previous six months:

Aggression Against People Or Animals

✔ Engages in frequent bullying or threatening

✔ Often starts fights

✔ Has used a weapon that could cause serious injury (gun, knife, club, broken glass)

✔ Has shown physical cruelty to people

✔ Has shown physical cruelty to animals

✔ Has engaged in theft with confrontation (armed, robbery, extortion, mugging, purse snatching)

✔ Has forced sex upon someone

Property Destruction

✔ Has deliberately set fires to cause serious damage

✔ Has deliberately destroyed the property of others (except for fire setting)

Lying or Theft

✔ Has broken into a building, car, or house belonging to someone else

✔ Frequently lies or breaks promises for gain or to avoid obligations ("conning")

✔ Has stolen valuables without confrontation (burglary, forgery, shoplifting)

Serious Rule Violation

✔ Beginning before age 13, frequently stays out at night against parents' wishes

✔ Has run away from parents overnight twice or more (once if for an extended period)

✔ Beginning before age 13, engages in frequent truancy

- These symptoms cause clinically important job, school, or social impairment.
- If older than age 18, the patient does not meet criteria for Antisocial Personality Disorder.

From American Psychiatric Association (1994). *Diagnostic and statistical manual of mental disorders, fourth edition*. Washington, DC. (pp. 90-91)

Appendix C:

Criteria For Oppositional Defiant Disorder

For at least six months, the patient shows defiant, hostile, negativistic behavior; four or more of the following often apply:

✔ Losing temper often
✔ Arguing with adults
✔ Actively defying or refusing to carry out the rules or requests of adults
✔ Deliberately doing things that annoy others
✔ Blaming others for own mistakes or misbehavior
✔ Being touchy or easily annoyed by others
✔ Being angry and resentful
✔ Being spiteful or vindictive

- The symptoms cause clinically important distress or impair work, school, or social functioning.
- The symptoms do not occur in the course of a mood or psychotic disorder.
- The symptoms do not fulfill criteria for Conduct Disorder.
- If older than age 18, the patient does not meet criteria for Antisocial Personality Disorder.

From American Psychiatric Association (1994). *Diagnostic and statistical manual of mental disorders, fourth edition*. Washington, DC. (pp. 93-94)

Appendix D:
Anger Disorders

Researchers, Christopher Eckhardt and Jerry Deffenbacher, described five basic anger disorders in the book, *Anger Disorders*, by Howard Kassinove, 1995, Taylor & Francis Publishing, Washington D.C.

Adjustment Disorder With Angry Mood

Characteristics would be a predominant manifestation of anger, such as periods of angry affect and irritability, becoming sullen, anger outbursts, or behavioral displays not sufficient to fit conduct problems, such as irritable complaining and becoming picky, snappy, making verbal or physical threats(but not acting on them), slamming objects, or throwing things. According to the DSM-IV, adjustment disorders are maladaptive reactions to identifiable psychosocial stressors that occur within three months after onset of the stressor, and have persisted for no longer than 6 months.

An example would be a child or adolescent that is sullen, argumentative, irritable, and angry with his/her parents for moving away from established friends, school, and neighborhood.

Situational Anger Disorder WITHOUT Aggression

This anger disorder describes a persistent (present 6 months or more), consistent, intense anger reaction to a circumscribed situation. Although the individual becomes demonstrably angry, he/she does not show significant aggressive behavior.

An example would be a sixth grader who gets very angry when students crowd ahead of his/her in lunch line. He/she may tense-up, get flushed in the face, curse internally, or complain to others. The child will not be aggressive.

Situational Anger Disorder WITH Aggression

This disorder involves both elevated anger and aggressive behavior in response to specific situations.

An example would be Lewis, a fifth grader, who is usually an easy-going person until he is put in an uncomfortable or irritable situation. During a pick-up game of basketball he gets fouled, preventing him from scoring. He gets angry and yells and starts hitting the other player.

General Anger Disorder WITHOUT Aggression

Whereas the situational anger disorders are circumscribed, the disorder describes the individual who is chronically and pervasively angry, but not highly aggressive. He/she always seems unhappy and/or irritable. The individual may occasionally behave aggressively, either verbally or against objects (e.g., make sharp comments, pout or sulk, slam doors).

General Anger Disorder WITH Aggression

Whereas the situational anger disorders are circumscribed, this disorder involves both frequent periods of generalized anger and frequent aggressive behavior. This disorder describes an individual who is frequently in an angry mood, but also does things such as engage in sarcasm, put others down, make verbal threats, or elevate discussions to loud arguments and yelling matches. For another individual, the mode of anger expression may be more physical than verbal.

Appendix E:

A Teacher's List of Do's & Don'ts On Medication

This list was devised with the help of Patricia Williford, School Psychologist

DO:

✔ Realize that behavior and academic performance may vary from day to day even with medication.

✔ Monitor behavior and academic performance while on medication with feedback given to parents, physicians and counselors. Use notes, phone calls, and behavioral rating scales.

✔ Maintain confidentiality with children on medication with peers and adults.

✔ Treat medication as a controlled substance. Consult school policy regarding storage and administration.

✔ Be watchful for any changes in behavior (i.e., insomnia, loss of appetite, constant thirst, diarrhea, nervousness, nausea, etc.) and in academics.

✔ Include counseling, academic, and behavior interventions along with the medication. Medication is not "the answer" or a "quick fix."

✔ Be conscious of consistent medication administration if given at school as directed by a physician. Inform parent when the amount of medication is running low.

✔ Be available to answer questions from students as it relates to medication and school/behavior issues.

DON'T:

✗ Expect a miracle or a perfect student following a medication intervention.

✗ Single out a student with peers or adults to get medication via the school intercom, reminders in front of class, posted notes, etc.

✗ Ask students, "Did you take your medication today?" When a difficult day is observed. (This gives the student an over reliance on medication as "fixing" his/her behavior or academics.)

Appendix F:

RECOMMENDED RESOURCES ON ANGER

AND RELATED TOPICS

Kassinove, H. (1995). *Anger disorders*. Washingon, D.C.: Taylor and Francis.

Green, R. (1998). *The explosive child*. New York: HarperCollins.

Shapiro, L. (1994). *Tricks of the trade*. King of Prussia, PA: Center for Applied Psychology.

The Misunderstood Emotion, 2nd edition, Touchstone, NY: 1989.

Wilde, J. (1996). *Treating anger, anxiety & depression in children and adolescents*. Philadelphia: Accelerated Development.

Williams, R. (1993). *Anger kills*. New York: Random House.

The following related resources can be ordered through
YouthLight, Inc. • P.O. Box 115 • Chapin, SC • 29036
1-800-209-9774 • Fax (803) 345-0888
email YLDR1@aol.com

Boatwright, B., Mathis, T., Smith-Rex, S. (1998). *Getting Equipped To Stop Bullying*.

Bowman, R.P, Johnson J.L, & Thomas-Williams, M. (1999) *Aggressive & Violent Students*.

Bowman, R.P, & Bowman, S. (1998). *The Chill Out Bag*.

Bowman, R.P, Cooper, K., Miles, R., Carr, T., & Toner, T. (1998). *Innovative Strategies for Unlocking Difficult Adolescents.*

Bowman, R.P, Cooper, K., Miles, R., Carr, T., & Toner, T. (1998) *Innovative Strategies for Unlocking Difficult Children.*

Braman Randall, O. (1997). *The Oppositional Child.*

Franklin Learning Systems, Inc. (1997). *Breaking the Chains of Anger.*

Franklin Learning Systems, Inc. (1997). *Meeting of the Minds.*

Eggert, L. (1994). *Anger Management For Youth.*

Kurcinka, Mary Sheedy (1998). *Raising Your Spirited Child: A guide for parents whose child is more intense, sensitive, perceptive, persistent, energetic.*

Romain, T. (1997) *Bullies Are A Pain In The Brain.*

Senn, D., & Sitsch, G. *Coping With Conflict: An Elementary Approach.*

Wilde, J. (1997). *Hot Stuff to Help Kids Chill Out.*

References...

Adorno, T.W., Frenkel-Brunswik E., Levinson, D.J., & Sanford, R.N., (1950). *The authoritarian personality.* New York: Harper.

American Psychiatric Association. (1994). *Diagnostic and statistical manual of mental disorders.* (Fourth Edition). Washington, DC.

Bloomquist, M. (1996). *Skills training for children with behavior disorders.* New York: Guilford Press.

Borcherdt, B. (1989). *Think straight, feel great!* Sarasota, FL: Professional Resource Exchange.

Buntaine, R., & Costenbader, V. (1997). Self-reported differences in the experiences and expression of anger between girls and boys. *Sex Roles, 36,* 625-637.

Carr, T. (1999). *Monday morning messages.* Chapin, SC: Youthlight.

Carr, T. (1996). *A parent's blueprint.* Chapel Hill, NC: Professional Press.

Coie, J.D., Lochman, J.E., Terry, R., & Hyman, C. (1992). Predicting early adolescent disorders from childhood aggression and peer rejection. *Journal of Consultation & Clinical Psychology, 60,* 783-792.

Comer, James P. (1988). Educating poor minority children. *Scientific American, 259,* 5.

Daldrup, R. (April 1989). How a good dose of anger therapy can restore peace of mind. *Personal Best,* 8.

DiGiuseppe, R. (1995). *Anger disorders.* Developing the therapeutic alliance with angry clients, edited by Kassinove, H., Washington, DC: Taylor and Francis.

Eckhardt, C., & Deffenbacher, J. (1995). Diagnosis of anger disorders, in *Anger Disorders,* edited by Kassinove. H. Washington, DC: Taylor and Francis.

Efran, J., Mitchell, & Gordon, D. (March/April 1998). Lessons of the new genetics. *Family Therapy Networker.*

Ekman, P., (1974). Universal facial expressions in culture and personality: *Contemporary Readings.* Chicago: Aldine.

Feshbach, N.D., & Feshbach, S. (1987). Affective processes and academic achievement. *Child Development, 58,* 1335-1347.

Garbarino, James (1999). *Lost boys.* New York: Free Press.

Glasser, W. (1984). *Take effective control of your life.* New York: Harper and Row.

Glasser, W. (1998). *Choice theory.* New York: Harper Collins.

Goleman, D. (1995). *Emotional Intelligence.* New York: Bantam Books.

Goodman, J. (1995). *Laffirmations: 1,001 ways to add humor to your life and work.* Deerfield Beach, FL: Health Communications, Inc.

Greene, R. (1998). *The explosive child.* New York: Harper Collins.

Hamer, D. (1998). *Living with our genes.* New York: Doubleday.

Harris, J. (1998). *The nurture assumption.* New York: Free Press.

Harvey, V. (1991). *Children and perfectionism.* Parent/Teacher Handout. National Association of School Psychologists.

Houston, B., & Vavak, C. (1991). Cynical hostility: Development factors. *Health Psychology, 10,* 9-17.

Huesmann, L.R., Eron, L.D., Lefkowitz, M.M., & Walder, L.D. (1984). The stability of aggression over time and generations. *Development Psychology, 20*, 1120-1134.

Huesmann, L.R., Eron, L.D., & Yarmel, P.W., (1987). Intellectual functioning on aggression. *Journal of Personality & Social Psychology, 52*, 232-240.

Johnson, R.J., & Kaplan, H.B. (1998). Gender, aggression, and mental health intervention during early adolescence. *Journal of Health & Social Behavior, 29*, 53-64.

Jones, F. (1987). *Positive classroom discipline*. New York: McGraw-Hill.

Kagan, J. (Sept./Oct. 1998). How we become who we are. *Family Therapy Networker*, 52-63.

Kassinore, H. (1995). *Anger disorders*. Washington, D.C.: Taylor & Francis Publishing.

Kessler, R. (Aug. 13, 1998). Harvard medical school study: *USA Today*.

Kohn, A. (1993). *Punished by rewards*. Boston: Houghton Mifflin.

Marion, M. (1994). Encouraging the development of responsible anger management in young children. *Early Child Development and Care, 97*, 155-163.

Mueller, C., Dweck C. (December, 1998). The right kind of praise. *Family Therapy Networker*, 601-611.

Neil, A.S. (1960). *A radical approach to child rearing*. New York: Summer-Hill.

Parker, J.G. & Asher, S.R. (1987). Peer relations and later personal adjustment: Are low-accepted kids at risk? *Psychology Bulletin, 102*, 357-389.

Preiebe, Phylis, Rudd, Shirley, and Lenthall, Nancy (December, 1993). The anger punch: An activity to vent anger in a positive way. *Practical Ideas for Counselors*, 7.

Purkey, William (1991). *Living and learning.* Washington, D.C.: National Education Association.

Reeder, D. M. (1991). Cognitive therapy of anger management: Theoretical and practical considerations. *Archives of Psychiatric Nursing, 3,* 147-150.

Rosemond, J. (January 31, 1999). *The Herald Sun*

Rowe, D. (1990). As the twig is bent: The myth of child-rearing influences on personality development. *Journal of Counseling and Development, 68,* 606-611.

Sears, S.J., & Milburn, J. (1990). School-age stress. *Childhood Stress,* edited by Arnold, E., New York: John Wiley and Sons.

Shapiro, L. (1994). *Tricks of the trade.* King of Prussia, PA: Center for Applied Psychology.

Skovholt, T. (August, 1990). Counseling implications of genetic research: a dialogue with thomas bouchard. *Journal of Counseling and Development,* 634.

Stoltz, P. (1997). *The adversity quotient.* New York: Wiley & Sons.

Tavris, C. (1989). *Anger: The misunderstood emotion,* 2nd Edition. Touchstone, NY.

Tavris, C. (1984). On the wisdom of Counting to ten. *Review of Personality & Social Psychology,* 170-191. New York: P. Shaver, Sage.

Trivedi, L. & Perl, J. (1995). Animal facilitated counseling in the elementary school: A literature review and practical consideration. *Elementary School Guidance & Counseling, 29,* 223-224.

Tyson, Janet (1998). *Common threads of grief.* Lake Dallas, TX: Helm Publishing.

Waas, G.A. (1987). Aggressive rejected children. *Journal of School Psychology,* *25,* 383-388.

Wegner, and Pennebaker. (1993). *Controlling anger: Self-induced emotion change: Handbook of mental control.* Englewood Cliffs, NJ: Prentice-Hall.

Wilde, J. (1996). *Treating anger, anxiety & depression in children and adolescents.* Philadelphia: Accelerated Development.

Williams, R. (1993). *Anger kills.* New York: Random House.

Woodard, J. (November, 1998). A personal encounter with the power of story telling. *Education Week,* 27.

Wright, W. (1998). *Born that way.* New York: Alfred Knopf.